Grateful Dead

A Headlands Press Book

Grateful Dead

The Official Book of the Dead Heads

Preface by Jerry Garcia

Paul Grushkin
Editorial

Cynthia Bassett
Design

Jonas Grushkin
Photography

QUILL

New York 1983

Produced by The Headlands Press, Inc., Tiburon, California.

Producer: Andrew Fluegelman

Text editor/permissions: Susan Brenneman

Cover illustration: Alton Kelley

Paste-up: Virginia Mickelson

Typography: Frank's Type, Mountain View, California and Solotype Typographers, Oakland, California

Reprography: Photopia, Mountain View, California

Color separation: Color Tech Corporation, Redwood City, California

Library of Congress number: 82-62276
82-62273 (pbk)

ISBN: 0-688-01917-X
0-688-01520-4 (pbk)

Printed in the United States of America

4   5   6   7   8   9   10

"Grateful Dead"®,   ("Skull with Lightning Bolt"), and

("Skull with Roses") are registered trademarks of Grateful Dead Productions, a California corporation.

The authors gratefully acknowledge permission to reproduce graphic art or reprint text from the following sources:

ARRIVAL: "Campers await 'The Dead'" by Paul McEnroe, *The Ann Arbor (Michigan) News,* October 9, 1979. Copyright © 1979 *The Ann Arbor News.* Reprinted by permission.   Letter to the editor, *Dead Relix,* September-October, 1975. Copyright © 1975 *Dead Relix,* 1734 Coney Island Avenue, Brooklyn, New York 11230. Reprinted by permission.   "No wait too long for 'Deadheads'" by Gail Tagashira, *San Jose (California) Mercury News,* December 31, 1978. Copyright © 1978 *San Jose Mercury News.* Reprinted by permission.   Franken and Davis quotation, *Dead Ahead.* Copyright © 1981 Grateful Dead Productions. Reprinted

by permission.   "Dead heads…They'll stand in long lines to buy Grateful Dead tickets" by Susan Jacobs, *The Southern Illinoisan,* January 30, 1979. Copyright © 1979 *The Southern Illinoisan.* Reprinted by permission.   "Winterland, '78 tonight go out in style with Grateful Dead" by David N. Rosenthal, Associated Press, *San Jose (California) Mercury News,* December 31, 1978. Copyright © 1978 Associated Press. Reprinted by permission.   "Take Me Out To The Rock Scene, Take Me Out With The Crowd, Buy Me A Kilo…" by Alan Edwards, *The Trenton (New Jersey) Times,* October 27, 1972. Copyright © 1972 *The Trenton Times.* Reprinted by permission.   "Grateful Dead Fans Won't Give Up The Ghost" by Jeff Meyers, *St. Louis Post-Dispatch,* July 13, 1980. Copyright © 1980 *St. Louis Post-Dispatch.* Reprinted by permission.   "Raised by the Dead" by Douglas E. Hadden, *The Boston Ledger,* September 18, 1980. Copyright © 1980 *The Boston Ledger.* Reprinted by permission.   "The Dead still soar" by Clint Roswell, *(New York) Daily News,* October 26, 1980. Copyright © 1980 New York News Inc. Reprinted by permission. "Dead's Followers Fiercely Loyal" by Rob Joseph, *(Buffalo, New York) Courier-Express,* November 9, 1979. Copyright © 1979 *Courier-Express.* Reprinted by permission.   "Dead Heads: A Strange Tale of Love, Devotion and Surrender" by Blair Jackson, *BAM,* April 4, 1980. Copyright © 1980 BAM Publications, Inc. Reprinted by permission.   "Grateful Dead give life to rock" by Wayne Crawford, *Chicago Daily News,* December 1, 1970. Copyright © Field Enterprises, Inc. Reprinted by permission.   "The Grateful Dead Are Rising Again" by Robert Christgau, *The New York Times,* July 27, 1969. Copyright © 1969 by The New York Times Company. Reprinted by permission.   "Fan plans eighth return to Dead" by Paul Levy, *The Minneapolis Star,* July 10, 1981. Copyright © 1981 Minneapolis Star and Tribune Company. Reprinted by permission.   "Grateful Dead" by Marty Schwarzbauer, *Willamette Valley (Oregon) Observer,* May 22, 1980. Copyright © 1980 *Willamette Valley Observer.* Reprinted by permission.   "Not Too Old to Rock and Roll" by Jeffrey A. Panzer, Timothy Cothren (producers), and Geraldo Rivera (correspondent), *20/20,* December 10, 1981. Copyright © 1981 American Broadcasting Companies, Inc. Reprinted by permission. Grateful Dead, Jefferson Airplane, Sons of Champlin poster by Bonnie MacLean Graham. Copyright © 1969 Bill Graham #197. Reproduced by permission.   "Grateful Dead: Still treading the

For Philip Grushkin,
Jane Eskilson,
Matt Chamberlain,
and Magnolia

(Continued on page 209)

v

Acknowledgements

This book was an opportunity to follow our hearts and document feelings that we ourselves share about the Grateful Dead. Everywhere we went—to the concerts, to the files, to the drawing board, to the darkroom—we were surrounded by exciting choices. The deeper we got into it, the more we saw revealed.

The years involved in making the selections dominated our lives and those of our families and friends. Now that we're at last finished, we hope everyone who helped and encouraged us will share in our joy and sense of accomplishment.

There are a *lot* of people to thank, foremost among them are the Grateful Dead themselves. Jerry Garcia, Phil Lesh, Bill Kreutzmann, Bob Weir, Mickey Hart, Brent Mydland, Robert Hunter—thank you for your confidence in our ability to tell the story. It is our greatest pleasure to present you with this book.

We also would like to remember Ron (Pigpen) McKernan and his influence, and the contributions of Keith and Donna Godchaux and Tom Constanten. To each member of the Dead, past and present, heartfelt thanks.

There are almost no words adequate to thank Eileen Law for her care and love. If there is any one person at the Dead's office who has believed in this book along with us, it is she. We also are very grateful to Alan Trist for developing our vision and bringing the project to the attention of the band. Warm support came as well from Rock Scully, Dicken Scully, Danny Rifkin, Carolyn Garcia (Mountain Girl), and Mary Ann Mayer.

Thanks must go to all the other members, past and present, of the Dead's staff and crew, including Dan Healy, Steve Parish, Bill Candelario, Ramrod, Rex Jackson, Joe Thomas, Paul Roehlke, Jeffrey Boden, John Cutler, Harry Popick, Willy Legate, Bob Matthews, Betty Cantor-Jackson, Sue Stephens, Janet Soto, Bonnie Parker, Carolyn (Goldie) Rush, Frances Carr, Zohn Artman, Julie Milburn, Jon McIntyre, and Richard Loren.

We are thankful to have merited the backing of William Morrow & Company and The Headlands Press. Andrew Fluegelman at Headlands piloted us past uncertain shoals and served effectively as our representative. We are also grateful for the leadership of editorial director Jim Landis at Morrow, and the help of production director John Ball and marketing director Al Marchioni. Thanks go to Hal Silverman, of *California Living* for interesting Morrow in the project.

Profound appreciation goes to Alton Kelley for creating the beautiful cover for our book. The clarity of our overall presentation is in no small part due to the skill and patience of text editor Susan Brenneman. Thanks also to Ginny Mickelson, Lori and Rick Reno, John Clifton at Keeble and Schucat Photographic (Palo Alto, California), John Gasser at Adolph Gasser Photographic (San Francisco, California), and the Zeiss-Ikon Voigtländer Contarex and Hologon photographic systems.

We hold a special place in our hearts for concert producer Bill Graham and his staff. Bill always comes through with more than anyone could expect, and we feel fortunate that he is our hometown impresario. Hats off to Bill Graham Presents staff members Peter Barsotti, Jan Simmons, Danny Scher, Sherry Wasserman, Bob Barsotti, Brian Auger, Steve Welkom, and all the dedicated people who work so hard behind the scenes.

We would like to credit John Scher and Monarch Entertainment for producing shows where many of our photos were taken, and also thank the staffs at Colorado's Feyline and San Francisco's Keystone Family for their support. A word of appreciation is also due Chet Helms and San Francisco's Family Dog.

The resources at the Bay Area Music Archives in San Francisco were indispensable, and we appreciate the encouragement of directors Dennis Erokan, Art Sohcot, and Miles Hurwitz. We also are grateful for the support (and Xerox machine) of David Rubinson and Friends, including D.R. himself, Vincent Lynch, and Brad Pueschel. Ned Hearn, our friend and legal counsel, worked hard on our behalf, and we also appreciate the help provided by Randy Sarti and Travel Advisors of Marin (San Rafael, California).

We worked closely with many poster collectors and rock music archivists. Postermat owner Ben Friedman's generosity must be noted first, for he dug into his legendary warehouse for us. Tim Patterson, whose personal collection is among the very best, was instrumental in locating many of the rarest pieces. We also are grateful to Gilbert Levey, Dennis King, Del Furano and Winterland, Cummings Walker and Berkeley Bonaparte, Wendy Sievert, Alan (Tex) Westerlund, Bill Hamilton, Edith Mirante, Bob Leonard, Phil Hammond, Bill Schuessler, and Eric King. Many thanks as well to all the poster artists and photographers whose work is included in the book, and thanks to everyone who sent material to the band's Dead Head office.

Many, many other people contributed help and special inspiration. In this regard, we would like to mention Ralph J. Gleason, John L. Wasserman, Michael Lydon, Joe McGinniss, Tom Wolfe, Jann Wenner and *Rolling Stone,* Alice Polesky, Joel Selvin, Blair Jackson and *BAM* magazine, Ripstop Rose, Tim and Lois Wachtel, Peter Simon, John Hamburger, Phil Elwood, Ben Fong-Torres, Jerry Horn, Les Kippel, Larry Bedard, Alec Levy, Bernie Bildman, Debbie Trist, Nicki Scully, Bear, Bill Walton, Peter Monk, John Barlow, Bobby Petersen, Merl Saunders, Gregory Redlitz at Kant and Starr (Los Angeles, California), Ren Grevatt, Dead Echoes, Julia Burch, Jacob the Chicago taxi driver, David Clarke, Dave Baker, Bob Nystedt, Bill Coe, Jim Lane, Rosie Mazet, Tom and Maggie Pinatelli, Laura Walsh, Sue Ruetz, Joe Ruetz, Kate Rosenbloom, Monte Stern, Ralph Brown, Karl Essig, Tom Funkhouser, Mike Cohan, and Chris Peck.

Our family and closest friends provided warm support throughout. We are especially grateful to Jean Grushkin, Dena Grushkin, James and Wilma Bassett, Peter Wing, Melinda Burch Wing, Alan Silverberg, and the Portola Valley house.

Concert tapers Jaime Poris, Bob Menke, and Dick Latvala provided special support, and good friends Lou Tambakos, Barbara Lewit, and David Gans sustained us over the long haul by virtue of their helpful criticism and high good humor. Dennis McNally, historian and soulmate, nourished us with inspiration. His dedication to the same muse set the highest possible standard for us to follow.

Bill Koch shared our vision from the beginning. When we needed a partner to sustain momentum in the early going, he was there.

The three people to whom we dedicate this book, along with our late family dog, are closest to our hearts. Phil, Jane, and Matt—thank you for putting up with the obsession this project imposed. Because you stood behind us, the incredible effort was worth it in the end. A big hug to each of you.

Although it's not possible to thank by name all the hundreds of people who contributed to this book, every one of them deserves a round of applause. Many thanks! See you at the next show.

Paul Grushkin, Cynthia Bassett, Jonas Grushkin

Contents

Preface

Back in 1965, some of my friends and I answered a Cosmic Want-ad for "mind expansion, the experimental life laboratory, continual musical education, socio-pharmaco-musicological adventures, and weird and wonderful trips." The response produced the Grateful Dead. Incredibly, it turned out there were lots of other people in the world who answered the same ad. They became the Dead Heads. All of us have a special relationship to the music which in turn behaves as if it has a mind of its own.

Around the time of the Human Be-In, when we were the neighborhood band—the acid band—someone came up to me after a show and said, "I remember you. You were at music school with me in Heaven." That cracked me up. It is typical of the one-liner exchanges I have had over the years with Dead Heads—a good-humored bunch who never allow us to take ourselves too seriously. It has been my entertainment to walk around and catch the humor of these characters and become *their* audience.

During the hiatus of 1975, while working on the Grateful Dead concert movie, I became familiar with a number of Dead Heads via the process of editing film. These characters, seen waiting on line or dancing in the crowd, became stars in the most direct kind of way, as much as I am to them at the other end of the spectrum. For me, making the film gave Dead Heads the opportunity to be larger than life—a state normally reserved for actors in the movies. I got autographs from some of them.

I see the Dead Heads both as familiar faces in the audience and stars in their own right. All of us involved in this reciprocal entertainment, including the authors of this book, know something about these things. *The Book of the Dead Heads* is a celebration of the whole set of relationships involved in this long, strange trip. I hope you are enjoying it as much as I am.

Jerry Garcia

Introduction

Grateful Dead, Haight-Ashbury, San Francisco, 1967. Photo by Herb Greene.

Hello Friends,

What is to be done to become a "Dead-Head"? What conditions must be filled up when entering your fan-club? Are there any contributions to be paid regularly? Is it true there must not be more than one "Dead-Head" in each town? What is the function of a "Dead-Head," and in what way must he take care of the other fans of the Dead-music?

I count upon your soon reply that will certainly contain the necessary data and formulas for accession.

In friendship,
Friedhelm Thamer

Dead Head letter
Meinerzhagen, West Germany, 1981

Dear Friedhelm,

What is to be done? Simply jump in and take part. After all, the experience of being a Dead Head begins whenever anyone turns on to Grateful Dead music for the first time. There are no rules, no application forms, and no fees except the price of a concert ticket. What's important is to go to Dead shows, enjoy the music in your own way, and share in the sense of community at a Grateful Dead concert. That is the "function" of a Dead Head and the "formula for accession."

The band provides the inspiration. Guitarists Jerry Garcia and Bob Weir, bassist Phil Lesh, drummers Bill Kreutzmann and Mickey Hart, keyboardist Brent Mydland, and songwriter Robert Hunter (a configuration that, save for the recent addition of Mydland and the death of vocalist Pigpen some years back, has remained basically intact for 18 years) are renowned for their classic songs and trademark improvisations. But it is the band *plus* the audience that creates a special experience, that turns a mere observer into a Dead Head.

At the very best Grateful Dead concerts, there is a compelling call and response that originates both on stage and out in the crowd. This unique partnership underlies the band's evolution beyond rock and roll and traditional American musical roots into the much higher realm of world folk song. *Melody Maker* magazine, in 1981, called it "a communion between equals, a true folk relationship in the sense that the band speaks *for* the audience rather than *at* them." To borrow a passage suggested to us by Phil Lesh from science fiction writer Theodore Sturgeon's 1953 book *More Than Human:* "There was happy and fearless communion, fearlessly shared—crosscurrents of humor, of pleasure, of reciprocal thought and mutual achievement. And through and through, *welcome, welcome."*

When a member of the Grateful Dead audience responds to that welcome, when he becomes a communicant and participates rather than just watches, when his voice is in balance with all the others—then for him the Grateful Dead come to life and he is on his way to becoming a Dead Head.

Since the band's inception in the 1960s, hundreds of thousands of people have experienced this change in their perception of the music. To use a vintage Dead expression, they've boarded the Grateful Dead bus. And although they've all gotten on the same bus, the way each person has walked through the door has been different. Each Dead Head has a story to tell, each has a unique way of describing and celebrating the first time it happened and all the times that followed.

It comes as no surprise that no other band in history has been represented by so many different T-shirts and concert costumes, carrying basically the same message. Much of this attire is homemade or unique in some respect, and certainly no one person could ever fit it all in one closet—there are literally hundreds of designs, old ones reemerging and new ones appearing on the scene each week. Under similar circumstances, dogma—a set of fixed beliefs dealing with a central object—might be a problem, but in Grateful Dead land, you are bombarded with myriad ideas and viewpoints, starting with the clothing.

What keeps the turning-on process alive and dynamic is that from person to person, show to show, nothing stays the same. The celebrated bus trip is invariably an excursion to "never ever land." The excitement lies in the discovery of what will happen next, and in what came before.

The taping phenomenon is instructive on this point. Each tape is different, just as each concert is different, just as each *listener* is different. What's on tape is the record of a unique situation, the particular balance on that occasion between the band's own interactions, the audience's degree of participation, and the acoustic feel of the room. All these variables mean there's always one more tape to trade for, to long for, to share with friends. No two tapes—and by extension, no two concert experiences—have ever been exactly the same.

The tapestry woven by all these memories and voices is colorful and vibrant. For the past five years it has held our fascination and prompted us to chronicle the evolution of this everflowing celebration. The result is as many stories and visions, images and versions as could be bound between two covers. Like the Dead concerts that it mirrors, *The Book of the Dead Heads* is a splendid mixture of dancers, tapers, costumed participants, and musicians. It is a portrait of a remarkable musical following in its own words and art, and it serves as a sort of guidebook, an invitation to jump in.

And it's been a matter of jumping in right from the beginning. In 1965, down on the peninsula south of San Francisco, near Palo Alto, Woodside, and Redwood City, California, a group of musicians jumped in and formed a band called the Warlocks, soon to be known as the Grateful Dead.

In the beginning, their only definable goal was to make music that people could dance to, but it was music that was also on the cutting edge of a larger social awakening. "Nobody was doing something, y'know, it was everybody doing bits and pieces of something, the result of which was something else," wrote Tom Wolfe in *The Electric Kool-Aid Acid Test.* "When it was moving right, you could dig that there was something that it was getting toward, something like ordered chaos, or some region of chaos."

The Dead's music has always embodied this sense of discovery. Even the first listeners felt the musicians' willingness to break with convention. The realization of new openness was a path-breaking experience, and to the adventuresome in the audience, it held an immediate, fascinating appeal.

Two of the first people to make a move in the band's direction were a couple of Beatlemaniacs named Connie Bonner and Sue Swanson. They become the first Warlock-fans turned Dead Heads. It was Sue, in 1967, who coined the phrase "The Golden Road to Unlimited Devotion," describing her and others' blossoming appreciation. (The band was so taken with her concept that they used the phrase to name one of the songs on their first record album.)

Some months before, in November, 1966 (a year after the Dead discovered their name in the Britannica World Language Edition of the *Funk & Wagnall's New Practical Standard Dictionary),* something else appeared that symbolized the growing bond between the band and the audience. This was the first official Grateful Dead T-shirt, the Pigpen shirt, honoring the charismatic bluesman who more or less fronted the band at that time. The following year, the Dead's first fan-club newsletter—*The Olompali Sunday Times*— and the first fan-club poster—the Alton Kelley/Stanley Mouse version of "The Golden Road"—appeared.

The Olompali Sunday Times, while short-lived, provided a glimpse of what life was like in San Francisco's Haight-Ashbury community, where the Dead were first perceived as an odd but lovable cultural institution. Wrote the newsletter staff, "Tourists come to look at the hippies, and the hippies come to see if tourists really come to look at them. People just looking at each other in the street on a beautiful, sunny afternoon, with nothing to do and nowhere to go.

"In an effort to make people happy by giving them something to do," the newsletter continued, "the Dead sometimes play unannounced in the Panhandle of Golden Gate Park on a flatbed truck to anybody who will come and listen to them. Needless to say, it's more interesting spending an afternoon in the park amongst the sun and trees than walking the crowded streets looking at each other."

With something as attractive as playing new music in a park (and at Bill Graham's Fillmore Auditorium, the Family Dog's Avalon Ballroom, and the Carousel, a musicians-cooperative dance hall), word spread rapidly that people should, to use an expression of the times, "dig the vibes" coming out of San Francisco. But what the Dead were doing was not easily labeled, and the more they toured, in California and then out of state, the more people they attracted on their own, on the basis of their unique musical style.

The albums—*Grateful Dead, Anthem of the Sun, Aoxomoxoa, Live Dead, Workingman's Dead,* and *American Beauty*—did much to cement their reputation. But even more important was the legend they established on the road. By 1969, they had caused a real stir in New York and throughout the East, and within another two years people all over America—from the 46th Street Rock Palace in Brooklyn to Springer's Ballroom in Portland—were turning on to the Dead in large numbers and swapping tales of fabulous concerts.

In 1971, Jerry Garcia had a suggestion. Maybe it was time to reach out and help the Dead Heads get in touch with each other. And so, printed inside the live double album *Grateful Dead* was this message:

DEAD FREAKS UNITE
Who are you?   Where are you?
How are you?
send us your name and address
and we'll keep you informed

The letters poured in from everywhere—all 50 states and many foreign countries. In early 1972, just prior to the band's first major tour of Europe, the Dead responded with the first official *Dead Heads Newsletter.* Bearing messages both diffuse and succinct, it provided the basis of an irregular pattern of keeping thousands of inquisitive souls up-to-date on the Grateful Dead.

"You probably have been wondering what it's all about… just as much as we have at times," the newsletter began. " 'Dead Heads' is not a fan club as such; we really don't think of it that way at any rate. We hope to be able to keep in contact with all of you, but the number of all of you seems to multiply far faster than we can accommodate your questions and requests. Originally, we had hopes of establishing some sort of communication system between all of you out there, but our own lack of money has prevented us from setting up something large and complex." In lieu of that, Garcia suggested: "Everyone ought to think of ways to get together with other Dead freaks. Don't hold your breath waiting for replies from us—that's the whole thing in this matter… don't hold your breath."

Until the band took a vacation from touring in late 1974, newsletters were sent out to an ever-growing mailing list as often as the Dead could afford to print and post them. And on the whole the relationship prospered. Via the newsletters, characters such as the mythical St. Dilbert appeared, and concepts like Hypnocracy evolved.

In fact, every possible aspect of the Grateful Dead-Dead Heads symbiosis was awarded scrutiny and comment. The contributions from the Dead Heads themselves were surprisingly coherent and much appreciated by the band and staff. "Your mail is an energy input—400 letters a week that we tack on bulletin boards and read aloud and pass back and forth," one early newsletter commented. "This flow enters the common pool of plans and theories and ideas and speculations and fantasies and hopes and fears and futures and galaxies and stuff. To hear from you, furthers."

The task of interpreting and channeling the messages to and from the Dead fell to two people in particular. Mary Ann Mayer headed up the Dead Heads office first, and later she was joined by Eileen Law, who serves in that capacity today. They devoted themselves to communicating with a rapidly expanding world of friends, and thanks to them the files of Dead Head correspondence, photos, and artwork were—and are—lovingly attended to. Because of Eileen's active participation, and that of Alan Trist, manager of the Dead's publishing company, and Rock Scully, in charge of the band's promotions, *The Book of the Dead Heads* contains many of the letters and clippings that the band themselves remember as striking.

By 1973, unchecked growth became a problem for the Grateful Dead. As one newsletter put it, "The pursuit of quality presentation of our music, with more and more people wanting to hear it, has led us into larger and larger halls with an ever-increasing array of equipment." The following year, in the final mailing of this series, the staff came right to the point: "People tire and you can only do one thing for so long. The band is weary of touring for ten years and needs to take a year and go fishing, because they really do. There's a scheme to keep the overall structure intact so there's something to take care of the details when the show goes back on the road. It is the fine response of Dead Heads over the years that leads us to conclude there's something worth maintaining, and that is what we're up to."

The vacation was a healthy one, and the Grateful Dead returned to regular action in the summer of 1976, a move hinted at by various cryptic communiques to the Dead Heads throughout the hiatus. Said one, "What was known as the Grateful Dead was dismantled, and the parts sent off for repairs. This is an operation a monster can sustain, which distinguishes him from an individual body." Said another, "Our first tour will be strictly to satisfy us and you and to find out if a smaller format can work. If it does, it can point the way to future tours that are a necessity for any band that

wants to stay at a dynamic level musically and serve as an energy source for itself and others."

For the most part, it's been that way ever since. While the newsletters have not been nearly as frequent as they were (replaced, to some degree, by the hotline phone numbers giving out the latest concert information), the volume of incoming Dead Head mail continues to be remarkable. Every letter is opened, the contents digested and important messages posted. The idea, still, is to keep everyone informed, somehow.

Several years ago we suggested to the Dead's staff that an effective way to carry on the process of sharing stories and feelings was to assemble this book, and to let as many people as possible contribute. In some cases people we had never met before, hearing of the project, took the time to write us with their observations.

One such new friend was Alan Mande, of Sausalito, California. "I first became a Dead Head in 1969," he wrote. "The Dead experience was powerful and cathartic. It triggered deep releases of emotional energy in me and in the audience around me. The whole community attended and left feeling purged and more attuned to their commonality.

"The Dead strike that resonant chord in everyone where passion and fervor are born. The community is scattered, so the band travels to us or we travel with them. The rituals are passed from person to person in a folklore concerning concert logistics and the trading of tapes. We gather in families and clans, everyone 'knowing' what's going to happen.

"The shared knowledge of songs and players' styles allows us to explore the synchronicity of a group mind at almost every concert. So of course the band doesn't have to *look* for an audience; we're *hungry* for this type of experience. Tell us where it's happening and we'll be there."

Becoming a Dead Head has everything to do with the times you're "there," the times you join in a circle of friends and families and experience the freedom of the Dead's music. Discovering your Dead Head identity means that you know when you've gone around the corner, when your disbelief melts into understanding.

It's as if your role as a member of the Grateful Dead audience is to serve as independent witness, to stand up and be recognized for knowing there's a special union taking place. If nothing else, this book serves as a record of those testimonials, those heartfelt declarations of belonging, those acknowledgements of an unspoken pact.

"We have seen the Dead and they are us!" proclaims a bumpersticker out in the parking lot. And what is done to be a Dead Head is the story of *all* our experiences.

In friendship,
Paul Grushkin, Cynthia Bassett, Jonas Grushkin

Kensington, Woodside, and Half Moon Bay, California
October, 1982

Arrival

◄ *Preceding page: Photo by Anna Moore*
*Butzner/*The Grand Rapids (Michigan) Press.

Old hippies never die—they just wait in line to see the Dead.

Paul McEnroe, The Ann Arbor (Michigan) News, *October 9, 1979*

The closing of Winterland in San Francisco, December 31, 1978. Photo by Dave Patrick.

Dear Relix People:

I was particularly interested in your "Ain't It Crazy" article. It brought to mind an incident at Watkins Glen. My friend lost his friend enroute to the Summer Jam. There's no way to locate anyone in a crowd of that size, so he decided to set up camp and enjoy the scene. The next morning the first person he saw, camping right beside him, was the friend he had lost hundreds of miles away! Ain't It Crazy?

Sue Berfer

Letter to the editor
Dead Relix, *September-October, 1975*

Four people arrived from Anchorage, Alaska, the same way they did last year and the year before that, without tickets but with the hope of getting lucky.

With sleeping bags, parkas, small portable heaters, chairs and bucket seats propped along the sidewalk, the cold didn't seem too bad on the streets.

Ruth Walker of Mountain View compared it to sleeping in the mountains, except for the loud traffic noises.

Gail Tagashira
San Jose (California) Mercury News, *December 31, 1978*

If all the people who've seen the Grateful Dead in concert stood end to end, the line would stretch all the way to the moon and halfway back.
And none of them would complain.

Franken and Davis
Dead Ahead *(videotape), 1982*

A blizzard was raging at 7:30 a.m., but the 150 "Deadheads" waiting outside the Southern Illinois University-Carbondale Arena for tickets to the Feb. 7 Grateful Dead concert were in high spirits.

The snow and wind Saturday didn't seem to bother these Grateful Dead fans. In fact, the Grateful Dead is a band that has drawn a group of followers that are so faithful, they call themselves "Dead heads."

Would they drive 100 miles for a Grateful Dead concert? "Sure," they say. Would they drive 200 miles? "Probably." Would they get up at 5 a.m. to wait in line? "Of course." Have they seen the band before? "Naturally."

Devotion knows no limits. "I've been here since 5 a.m. and it's been snowing all night," Paul Raemont, a junior at SIU-C, said. Although the box office would not open until 8 a.m., Raemont came early "to party with the people."

Susan Jacobs
The Southern Illinoisan, *January 30, 1979*

Bill Graham:
Dead fans are so loyal, "they come underwater, from Utah, backwards, to stand in line to see them play."

To David N. Rosenthal, Associated Press
San Jose (California) Mercury News, *December 31, 1978*

Left and above: One of the great waits. The line for tickets to the Radio City Music Hall shows, New York, October, 1980. Photos by Associated Press/World Wide.

There's a married couple in their fifties, waiting in line. The man is balding, graying, wears a zipped-up jacket, serious shoes, well-creased pants. There's a camera slung across his chest. His wife is small and gushy.

The line, two or three deep, swells into chaos where the couple stands—there are a lot of teenagers hanging around listening to what the man and woman are saying. There is sporadic laughter from the group, and each time it erupts, the man looks proud and the woman beams. Young people are so nice!

She continues: "Oh yes, I remember when we saw Santana at the Electric Factory about three years ago. It was a night as cold as this one. They were very good, with all those drummers and so on. And then there was the Grateful Dead…"—her audience sighs appreciatively—"We liked them so much!"

Alan Edwards
The Trenton (New Jersey) Times, *October 27, 1972*

Arrival **5**

Dead Heads follow their heroes around the country and blow into towns like a three-ring circus. "We just like to have a good time, listen to the Grateful Dead, do some acid and smoke a little pot," said Paul Conlon, 25, a Chicago cook who planned his vacation around the band's summer tour.

It is estimated that 300 or 400 Dead Heads are making the nine-city tour with the band. After a few days, faces become familiar, strangers turn into friends and maybe even lasting relationships are made. Roger Engel of Libertyville, Ill., met Sara Hudson of Amarillo, Texas, July 1 at the concert in Fort Worth. They've been together ever since. "We feel like we're part of a family," Hudson said, looking starry-eyed at Engel. "We've been with the same people now for over a week, and they're all beautiful."

Twenty-three of the Dead Heads chipped in $75 apiece, and converted an old school bus into a four-wheel motel sans toilet facilities. Accommodations were cramped and rank, to be sure. "We've had a few arguments," said Conlon. "It's hard for that many people to be together for so long (10 days so far). The trip hasn't been easy, either. The weather was really hot in Texas and one night we had to drive 500 miles without sleep to get to the next concert. We've had a money problem, too, basically because we only get five miles to the gallon. We've had to sell tie-dyed T-shirts and stickers to pay for our tickets and food and gas."

The driver of the bus, Jay Harris, was accompanied by his pet pit bull, Andre. The dog was making his second tour. "This is what's happening now, in the '80s," said Harris. "It's real, not nostalgia." Said Marvin Bellows of Carlinville, Ill. "It's the concerts that make the Dead what they are. If you catch the right concert, the band takes control of your mind, opens it up and the music pours in."

Jeff Meyers
St. Louis Post-Dispatch, *July 13, 1981*

There's a ritual courtesy among Dead fans, part legend, part real. The first time I heard the Dead in their own West Coast environment, I stood in line beforehand without a ticket, with friends who long before had bought theirs to the "Bill Graham Presents" bash at Winterland in San Francisco. "Are you guys sure I'll get a ticket?" I asked my friends. "Ticket?" said a bearded fellow two folks in front of me. Yup. And 5½ hours and the New Riders and a Grace Slick guest appearance later, the five bucks was forgotten, and the courtesy of a ticket for face value was not.

Douglas E. Hadden
The Boston Ledger, *September 18, 1980*

Photo by Betty Udesen/The Springfield (Oregon) News.

One of the fans who was celebrating the return of the Dead to New York is a 31-year-old Brooklyn cabby named Jeff Cohen. He hadn't expected to see the Dead on opening night, Wednesday, since he had been shut out of the Ticketron sales. He had been waiting thirteen hours at the Main St., Flushing, office for seats when he was apprised that only the first 113 people could be allotted tickets. Jeff was No. 123 on line, and as he waited all night on line, the possibility of not seeing the group never dawned on him.

When he was shut out, he cursed the fates and swore to get even. He drove over to Radio City Music Hall. The lanky, long-haired, denim-clad lad was pleasantly surprised. Due to the overwhelming demand, the box office had offered two new dates. Jeff joined a short line and got tickets for both nights. He traded some of the extras to get seats to other shows and will attend five of the eight nights.

"I could sell them for a good profit, but they're priceless," he said, a permanent smile planted on his face. "The Dead give me hope that all is not lost; they are an inspiration to me."

Clint Roswell
(New York) Daily News, *October 26, 1980*

The thousands "out there" who come to hear are often, like the band members themselves, living their lives somewhere removed from the mainstream. They hold jobs; they eat and sleep; but if the Grateful Dead are performing anywhere within a 500-mile radius of home, they drop everything to seek the music.

Rob Joseph
(Buffalo, New York) Courier-Express, *November 9, 1979*

I NEED A MIRACLE

in the form of a ticket for either of the **GRATEFUL DEAD** Warfield shows (Feb. 16 & 17). I was on the mountain sunshine day-dreaming while tickets (unknowingly to me) were selling out! Please answer this **DEAD**-icated and desperate plea if you have a ticket for me!

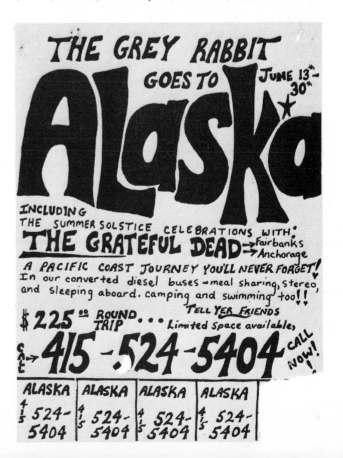

THE GREY RABBIT GOES TO Alaska JUNE 13th-30th

INCLUDING THE SUMMER SOLSTICE CELEBRATIONS WITH THE GRATEFUL DEAD → Fairbanks → Anchorage

A PACIFIC COAST JOURNEY YOU'LL NEVER FORGET! In our converted diesel buses — meal sharing, stereo, and sleeping aboard. camping and swimming too!!

$225.00 ROUND TRIP ... Limited space available,

TELL YER FRIENDS

S.E. → 415-524-5404 CALL NOW!

ALASKA	ALASKA	ALASKA	ALASKA
415 524-5404	415 524-5404	415 524-5404	415 524-5404

"There was *never* a possibility that we wouldn't go see the Dead in Egypt. We were going to do whatever it took... and we did." Larry Murcer of Portland, Oregon is sitting on top of a muddy sleeping bag in a park across the street from the Oakland Auditorium, where the Grateful Dead will ring in the New Year—1980—in about three hours. With his girlfriend Judy Schweiger, Larry hitched down to Oakland the day after Christmas and had been camping out in the park ever since with about 50 other Dead Heads. The Grateful Dead were playing five shows at the Auditorium, and Larry and Judy were

not about to let inconveniences like torrential winter rains and no money for food keep them from missing a single note of any of the performances. "I've been to every West Coast Dead show since mid-'77," Larry beams, the white of his teeth suddenly dominating his overwhelmingly furry countenance, "but Egypt was IT!"

When Larry first heard the reliable

rumors that the Dead were going to play a series of concerts at the foot of the Great Pyramid in September 1978, he quit his job as a parttime postal employee, sold all of his records ("even my Dead records—*that's* how important this was"), his stereo and his ten-speed bike and, with Judy, started hitching across the country.

Larry, Judy and four traveling companions flew to Cairo three days before the concerts, "scored THE BEST HASHISH I'VE *EVER* SMOKED," Larry bubbles, and managed to find a reasonably clean room in a private home, where the six of them stayed for the equivalent of 25 cents a day. By the day of the first show, Larry and the group had encountered dozens of other Americans, many of whom had gone to

them squares necessarily, or even imply that they're anything less than hardcore Dead Heads. After all, many were lined up to see their fifth Dead show in six days (*the band* took a day off) and many of them were attending their 30th, 40th, 80th, 150th, *225th* Dead concert, and if that's not hardcore, nothing is. Some of them undoubtedly staged bizarre rituals of their own those three nights the Dead were shattering the desert calm in Giza—listening to favorite Dead concert tapes in their homes in San Francisco, Seattle, Syosset, Long Island or wherever; filling rooms with suspicious-smelling smoke; and perhaps ingesting mysterious chemicals as they invoked the spirits of Osiris, Keb, Ra, Ptah, Anubis and

all the other deities awoken from their slumber by the Good Ol' Grateful Dead. Perhaps what the Dead Heads who didn't go to Egypt lacked was the *crazed* edge that separates the faithful from the *obsessed*—those poor souls who *had* to go, who seemingly had no choice in the matter because they were pulled by forces far too powerful to control. They're the Dead Heads whose eyes look right through you, who grin a toothy, just-this-side-of-diabolical smile that says, "I *know* something you can't even imagine." And they probably do.

Blair Jackson
BAM, *April 4, 1980*

similarly extreme lengths to make the Egypt trip. "One guy from Chicago figured out how to embezzle money from his *father's* business to get there," Larry claims.

"I'm not saying the Egypt shows were the *best* Grateful Dead concerts I've been to," Larry says, "They weren't. But they were definitely the *highest!* C'MON, man! THE DEAD... in *EGYPT!*" He breaks into a staccato laugh, and Judy hugs him. The Dead in Egypt. Be there or be square.

Most of the people in line at the Auditorium this New Year's Eve didn't make it to Egypt, which doesn't make

Photo by Ray Ballar.

Photo by Chuck Pulin.

Fire on the Mountain

It started in the Southwest with a show at Tempe, Arizona. Then Lois and I spent two extremely nice days up in Boulder. Then we were off to the Northwest and it was Portland, Seattle, and Spokane. The usual airplane ride, except that a few people mentioned how nice it would be if the Dead were to play "Fire on the Mountain" sometime on the tour because that's where Mt. St. Helens had erupted recently and everybody thought, Oh how ironic that would be, hurrah hurrah. We arrived early at the Portland show and mingled with the people on line. It was raining, but somebody got out a plastic tarp and we played tapes and laughed and had a great time until the doors opened. We got excellent seats (two nice rows of chairs), and people set up their taping gear and got ready.

I think the Dead came on early, around 7:30, played till 8:30 or so, took only a half-hour break, and got back on stage around 9:00. Now ordinarily the Dead have a basically standard approach to these second sets; as you know, they break two or three single songs and then they play a couple of extended pieces with lots of jamming and then some drums and then some more jamming and then, um, maybe a rock song or two and then a Garcia slow song and then Weir comes in and sees what he can do to get everybody up and shouting. This night they decided to do something a little different. They *started out* with some drumming, which they've done on only a few occasions, and then Jerry started into the notes of "Scarlet Begonias."

The Dead played a *spectacular* version of "Scarlet" and we were having a wonderful time dancing, and then they went into "Fire on the Mountain." Everybody cheered and thought how it was really great to be hearing "Scarlet" into "Fire on the Mountain," as here we are in Portland and so close to the mountain that blew up not three weeks before. Everybody officially observed the ironic circumstances and danced and clapped and enjoyed the hell out of it. The band continued to play their way through a pretty standard remaining set, and my only real memory is that it felt compressed, like the Dead were anxious to get off the stage. But there was no premonition of anything.

So we exited the place, and what *is* this? I'm walking out to my rented car and there is all kinds of dust coming down out of the sky. And falling on my head and everywhere and I'm thinking, *What* is going on? I went into the local Tic Toc and there was a television and a newscaster was reporting from the mountains about there being a state of emergency in mid-Oregon and how Mt. St. Helens had erupted for the second time at something like ten minutes after 9:00. *Mt. St. Helens,* of course! That would explain why…and then I thought, *9:10,* now wait a minute. The Dead came out at 9:00, and then the drums, and then "Fire," around 9:10. Wow, that *is* ironic! Well, I asked the guy at the counter, what's going to happen here now that we've got this doggone ash falling out of the sky, you know, I mean we've got to go see the Dead in Seattle tomorrow. He laughed at me, and the people who were in the Tic Toc laughed, being residents, and said, "You can just forget that buddy, 'cause you are stuck here in Portland and the last time we had this the

roads were closed so you can just plan on enjoying yourself with all these good folks, pal."

I talked to Lois and said this was going to be extremely bad. We did not want to be on the wrong side of a Dead concert under any circumstances. And she totally agreed and we went to the motel and loaded all our gear into the car. It was about 1:00 in the morning and the ash was coming down like mad. But we were on our way to Seattle, and a light rainfall was making a mud all over the car and we were laughing and we turned on the radio and every station had an ash report. So we got the tape player out and rewound back to "Fire on the Mountain" and cranked that sucker up and down the road we went.

We just made it over the bridge to exit Portland when I heard from another driver that the Portland Bridge had been closed! I breathed a sigh of relief, although I was really a little concerned because we could not see the road. The only way to tell you were changing lanes was by feeling the dots in the road. The visibility was maybe five to ten feet, and the traffic was *crawling* along the road and the ash was just going mad around us. It was very, very spooky, but we managed to use the Dead tapes we brought with us to great advantage.

It was an enlightening experience and would have been even better had we not run out of windshield wiper fluid.

Many's the time we crunched from a snail's pace down to a dead stop and sat and wondered what we were doing out in the middle of this. But it was basically an enlightening experience, and would have been even better had we not run out of windshield wiper fluid. I was forced to stick my left hand out and make temporary holes on the windshield, which meant we were driving blind for a good stretch. Finally, we passed Mt. St. Helens and the worst was over. We made it to a service station and hosed everything down—except for a patch on which we scrawled "Fire on the Mountain—We love the Grateful Dead!" We went on to see the show in Seattle—which was outrageous—and then on to Spokane for more, and the Dead ended things for us with a "Goin' Down the Road Feelin' Bad," which was certainly appropriate for this leg of the tour.

Only now, sitting on top of my tape collection at home is a little urn, and people always ask who died, and I say, well, it's a long story—what's the weirdest way you arrived at a Dead concert?

Tim Wachtel
1982

When the Dead come to town, it's like a statesman returning to his people.

Wayne Crawford
Chicago Daily News, *December 1, 1970*

ASK FOR REALTOR BOB WEIR

DEADHD NEW HAMPSHIRE

THE DEAD CALIFORNIA

CALIFORNIA HES GONE

DARKSTAR NEW YORK

CALIFORNIA IM DEAD

JERRY G NEW YORK

Photo by David Gans.

GRATEFUL DEAD

Gratefully Dedicated

NOTHINGLEFTTODOBUT SMILESMILE SMILE

The Only GOOD HEAD a DEAD HEAD

AINT NOTHING LIKE THE HEAD

Jerry Garcia:
"We get hard fans. Once we play the same place three or four times we know we have a core of fans that'll stay with us no matter what we do."

To Robert Christgau
The New York Times, *July 27, 1969*

The Dead are back in town. Where did I put my bells?

Patt, Big Times, *November 15, 1973*

Photo by Dave Patrick.

Photo by Richard McCaffrey.

They were scattered all around the St. Paul Civic Center: A few marijuana roaches here, a few beer cans there and even a tattered rose on the sidewalk. Taped to the building were several signs saying "G.D. Line Here."

This was May 11, two months before tonight's Grateful Dead concert at the Civic Center. The ticket buyers had begun arriving in the wee hours of the morning.

By about 11:30 a.m.—90 minutes after tickets had gone on sale—there couldn't have been more than 40 people waiting ahead of me. The guy directly in front—a silver-haired gent in a three-piece suit—began mumbling aloud.

"Wonder how long the concert will last?" he said to nobody in particular.

"They'll play till at least midnight," somebody said. "The Dead are always good for three or four hours."

"Last time I saw them," said somebody else, "they did two sets. Lasted six hours. That was at Red Rocks [near Denver]."

The silver-haired man smiled.

"I'd like them to play all night," he said. "You know, I haven't seen the Dead for eight months. But I've got to drive to Wisconsin the next day. They're playing at Alpine Valley, and I'm going with my kids and…"

Another voice cut in.

"Need some speed?" a guy, maybe 25, asked.

The silver-haired guy laughed heartily. "'Livin' on reds, vitamin C and cocaine,'" he said, quoting famous Dead lyrics from "Truckin'."

And, as if on cue, at least half a dozen strangers sang in unison, "'Ain't it a shame.'"

Paul Levy
The Minneapolis Star, *July 10, 1981*

They're the only band in the world who don't have to worry about adapting to the times. They're dragging the times along with them.

Marty Schwarzbauer
Willamette Valley (Oregon) Observer, *May 22, 1980*

Photo by Richard McCaffrey.

Jerry Garcia:
"Our audience is like people who like licorice. Not everybody likes licorice, but the people who like licorice really like licorice."

To Geraldo Rivera
20/20, December 10, 1981

Jerry Garcia:
"The fact that we still have an audience is incredible. The fact that we ever had one is incredible. The fact that we still have one and, further, that it's growing—all these things are very surprising."

To Dale Adamson
Houston Chronicle, *January 7, 1979*

THE GRATEFUL D
DANCE
PLUS
AUC
Wo

A PINNACLE SH
ADVANCE TICKETS $5
$5.50 AT THE DOOR.

OUTDOORS ON THE GRASS

GRATEFUL DEAD
NEW RI
OF THE PUR

UC-SANTA BARBARA
TICKETS $4.50 UCSB STUDENTS
LOMPOC MUSIC BOX, CAL POL
STEREO INFO BOOTH, SANTA MA
U. CEN. INFO BOOTH—SANTA BARBARA
ODYSSEY—SANTA MA
MERCANTI
LIMITED

A few days before the new year, 1980, the lobby floor at the Oakland Auditorium, in California, collapsed under the weight of too much "Truckin'."

Bob Weir:
"We tend to draw a different kind of person—someone with an advanced sense of adventure."

To Andrew Frances
Us, *August 5, 1980*

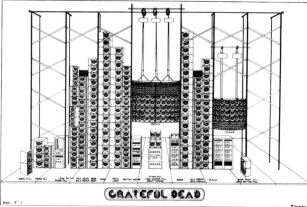

A schematic of the Dead's 1974 sound system.

Photo by Mary Ann Mayer.

It's something special.

It starts in the feet and builds. The legs get ready for what will certainly be a long night; and in the stomach—anticipatory butterflies. Then, it works its way to the most important set of muscles on each anatomy—it swirls around the brain awhile, until it comes out in the only logical solution:

You smile.

A universal smile, as you look around you at the people. It's finally time for that rampant bliss that will dominate the next seven hours. In a word, the *joy* of a Grateful Dead concert.

Tom Reed
(Walnut Creek, California) Contra Costa Times, *October 20, 1980*

THEATRE
MAY 21, 1982

BILL GRAHAM PRESENT

®

GRATEFUL DEAD

BACKSTAGE

CAPITOL THEATER
PASSAIC, N.J.

JUNE 18, 1976

Feyline
PRESENTS, INC

GRATEFUL DEAD

Compton Terrace
July 25
Red Rocks
July 27, 28, 29
Starlight
August 3

backstage

GRATEFUL DEAD

BACKSTAGE

FALL CONCERT
SEPT 30, 1972
BACKSTAGE
PASS

AUGUST 31, 1981
Theatre Las Ve

Bill Graham P
GRATEFUL
5 days · Oakland

VIDEO N

1981 "Here today,

GRATEFUL DEAD
THE BAND
BACKSTAGE
ROOSEVELT STADIUM

"The Dead are just, I don't know, man," said a 29-year-old construction worker named Tony Kryoski, a ponytail hanging below his hard hat. "They're an American institution."

"The Dead have been going on strong for 15 years," said Will Amrein, a 32-year-old Glenelg printer who runs Grateful Graphics. He has been following the band since 1968 and has seen it more times than he can remember.

"Can you describe Oriole magic, Oriole fever? No. That's what the Grateful Dead are.

"I'll be there tonight, waiting at the door, trying to get in. I'm not a sickie Dead Head," he warned. "I'm not A-a-a-h [he made a gutteral noise]. I've seen some of those A-a-a-h Dead Heads at the shows. It's just a good time for me; it's nothing serious."

David McQuay
Baltimore News American, *May 4, 1980*

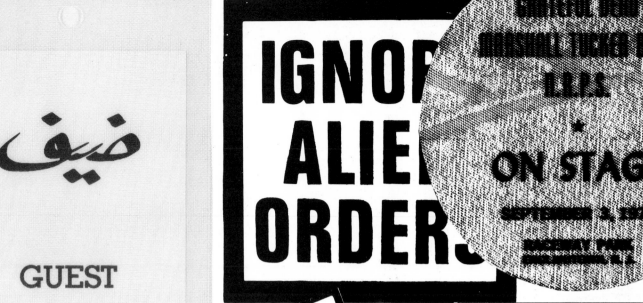

ضيف

GUEST

IGNOR
ALIE
ORDERS

GRATEFUL DEAD
MARSHALL TUCKER BAND
N.R.P.S.
*
ON STAGE
SEPTEMBER 3, 1977

nts
EAD
ditoriu
tomorrow" ·1982

28./29. März 1981 · Grugahalle Essen
WDR
Festival
Rockpalast
BACK STAGE
GRATEFUL DEAD

BACKSTAGE

Red Rocks
MORRISON, COLORADO
JULY 8, 1978

There was the predictable hassle at the
gate—our names weren't on the list, somebody from some congressman's office
wanted six tickets, and so forth—but we got
in eventually, which was also predictable.
The music was underway, but there was no
rush because there never is. Nadine and I
pushed and excused our way through the
crush up front to claim our seats, which
were relinquished cheerfully by a couple
who immediately occupied the aisle. Jollity
prevailed. The guy in front of me extended
his greetings on the basis of our Dead
T-shirts, which were similar. A woman
behind me extended greetings on the
basis of our T-shirts, which were identical.
Someone had given her hers in Vermont.

Robert Christgau
Newsday, *July 30, 1972*

BGP

SEPT 12, 1981

BILL GRAHAM PRESENTS

Dear Grateful Dead, keepers of the flame, gotta light?

8:07 a.m.—alarm goes off, immediately ingest 50 mg. uncut LSD-25. Go back to sleep before eyes open.

9:46—eyes open because things are getting too intense on the eyelids. Notice that blanket has turned into Cheryl Tiegs, smile, put on *Aoxomoxoa*. Crawl into bathroom, attempt to swim laps in the bathtub. Take 37 bong hits and find a juicy Vantage Light butt under the refrigerator. Forget to light it.

10:22—phone rings, forget which room you left it in. Put on *Workingman's Dead*, find tele-phone in the aquarium, agree to meet Ron at the Aristocrat in half an hour. Space on hologram-metaphysics, run through "Friend of the Devil" on guitar without a G-string, wonder where you left the mescaline. Smile again. You remember you've got field tickets and were supposed to go over to Folsom when the alarm went off. First wave of panic.

10:58—can't find *Steal Your Face*, now sweating profusely. Bacon turned into green lizards at the 'Crat, had to leave before the little fat men…never mind. Roommate is playing the Clash again, where's *Seastones* when you really need it? Find mescaline in backpack, eat it all to counter-act acid. Merely complicates geometry of reality. Consumes 47 times its weight in excess…wonder if you'll get a guitar pick from Jerry today, decide to wear the *Blues for Allah* jersey. Look for car keys. Take short detour through the Roger Dean mural. The Clash sound like an electric garage door trying to kill democracy. Must run away.

11:30—get halfway before you remember that this concert *isn't* at Red Rocks. Second wave of

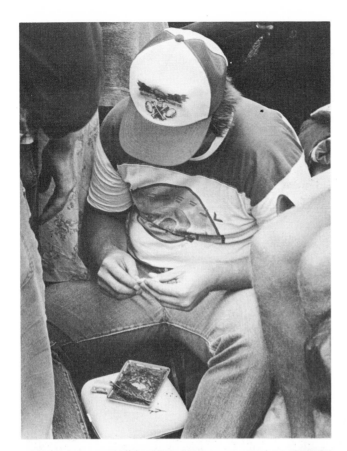

"The crew that goes to Grateful Dead shows is a special brand," said Don Posner of the Bronx. "They don't screw around. They just do their drugs and enjoy the music."

Associated Press
The (Palo Alto, California) Peninsula Times-Tribune, *September 24, 1980*

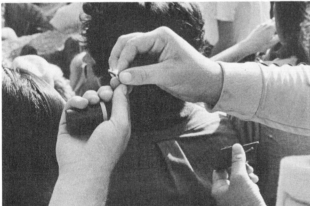

panic. Opening second pack of cigarettes as you realize you were supposed to pick up Sheila too. *Heaven Help the Fool* jams in the tapedeck, begin having nervous breakdown, swerve to avoid 280-ZX passing joggers. Cop roars up behind you, lights mesmerizing you. Pull over near Rocky Flats, eat three joints. Cop roars by. Faint.

12:02 p.m.—sprint to stadium. Get to gate, realize you forgot your ticket in the car.

Chris Clark
Colorado Daily, *June 7, 1980*

First Set

The Dead cast its first numbers onto the throng quietly, as if to invoke a special flame from a sacred lamp.

Dale Anderson
Buffalo (New York) Evening News, *September 27, 1973*

My initiation came in the winter of '72 in Wichita, Kansas. Strong grass and live Dead put me into a stoned trance, staring at Garcia. Something popped in my mind as I realized he was also staring at me. I beamed a huge uncontrollable grin at him. He winked back and jerked his guitar neck at me twice. I felt bolts of energy strike me, and my grin was fixed in place for the rest of the concert. I've been a Dead Head ever since. My mother will never understand.

Alan Praskin
Dead Relix, *January-February, 1976*

The sight was mass movement. Thousands of bodies, writhing, wiggling, seething, sizzling, but always without let up, constant, unceasing motion. The sound was a roar, always deafening, at times more deafening than others, but never less than loud. The smell was pot. It was faint at first, but always unmistakable, growing ever stronger.

The banners were going up all over the place. You counted 15 hanging from the second tier alone. They were masking taped up there, banners made of bedsheets and tablecloths and drapery, drawn in magic marker and tempera paints, all vowing devotion to a special rock group: Grateful Dead '78, God Bless the Grateful Dead, Long Live the Dead, There's Nothing Like a Grateful Dead Concert.

And as time moved forward, the roar grew louder, the movement more intense, the smell of pot stronger, until, when the house lights dimmed and finally blinked out, more than 19,000 kids exploded in a speeding, roaring, spaced-out gesture of cosmic goodwill.

Now you noticed some pretty strange goings on. A guy wearing an Uncle Sam outfit, another sporting a foot-long paper mache mask of something, still another dressed like a rat—ears, tail and all—with a bulbous, red, plastic clip-on nose. There was a group with skull decals stuck onto the middle of their foreheads.

And then there was Rick Rickards. He was carrying a bamboo pole with a human skull bolted onto the end. At least, from a distance, it sure looked human. "Naw," said Rickards, 18, from Doylestown and a student at Central Bucks East, "it's only plastic, like the ones they have at Halloween.

"See, I got it at K-Mart during a blue-lite special. You can always tell a Dead Head because if I shake it like this," he shook it up and down, "they'll start shouting and clapping and dancing around."

Bruce Olds
Bucks County (Pennsylvania) Courier Times, *January 7, 1979*

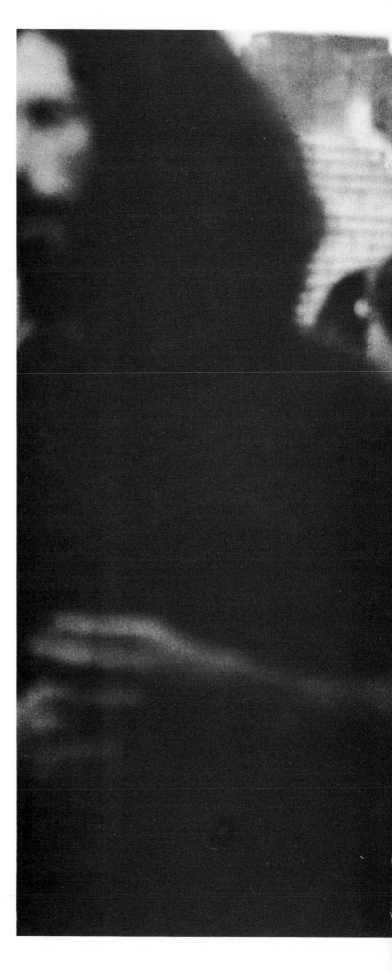

If there were any doubts as to where I was, they were immediately dispelled when the wiry young man with the crazed glaze came up to me with a plateful of bright red fruit and asked if I'd like an electric strawberry.

Jay Trachtenberg
The Daily Texan, *July 6, 1981*

The instant the sound was right the crowd was on its feet dancing.

C.B. Geanious, The (Oregon State University) Daily Barometer, November 2, 1981

The Dead at the Golden Gate Park Panhandle, San Francisco, circa 1966.   Photo by Jim Marshall.

First Set Notes
by Paul Grushkin

Wow
back again!
cheerful, expectant bedlam
as we sweep into the concert
fifty states
plus several foreign countries
an enormous rush of bodies
establishing territory
setting up shop
we unwrap, slowly s-t-r-e-t-c-h
and absorb the pre-Dead vibe
note pad out, friends all around
looks to me
like it's pretty damn amazing
hippies and freaks everywhere
young and old, stoned and straight
embracing one more time

houselights dim

everyone presses forward
God, what a noise!
utter synchronous din
unbelievably loud
such a joyous, ecstatic greeting
hello Grateful Dead
and the Dead are upon us!
ghostly, saintly figures
moving quickly into position
some tuning, a bit of laughter
and *wham*
there it—
here we
go!

"ONE MORE SATURDAY NIGHT"

whooooooooooooo!

can you *believe* this beginning?
man, just *listen* to this band
what a great crowd here tonight

shivering in stony pleasure
sheets of sound raining down

GET PREPARED
THERE'S GONNA BE
A PARTY TONIGHT

we howl in appreciation
yeah, turn it up
crank it, man—we can take it!
The Dead so sharp and daring
Garcia rootin', tootin'
Weir so full of spunk
such a treat!
sheer energy madness
go for it, you guys!

into "BERTHA"

yeeeeeeeeeooooooooowwwwwwww!!

I HAD A HARD RUN
RUNNIN' FROM YOUR WINDOW

BerthaBerthaBertha!

A concert in Golden Gate Park, September 28, 1975. Photo by Dave Patrick.

melody of pure dance
a roaring musical wind in our faces

TEST ME TEST ME
WHY DON'T YOU ARREST ME?

Lesh lets go with a sonic blast
the audience instantly responds
the love vibe, the sex beat
so ridiculous, yet so apparent
everyone knows it
no one can say what it is

THAT'S WHY IF YOU PLEASE
I AM ON MY BENDED KNEES

up red lights everywhere
a real rabble-rouser tonight!
folks *flinging* themselves skyward

ANY MORE
ANY MORE HOR HOR
ANYMORE!

into "GREATEST STORY
EVER TOLD"

classic!
one of Weir's all-timers
watch him take that mike
time for some shouting, Bobby!
and some guitar slashing
a band of warriors
American samurai
ripping and gutting with their axes
touching off explosions in my brain
how high can they go with this?
flash-point screams
white lightning bombardment
earth-shattering cascades
incredible chaos

SAID YOU CAN'T CLOSE THE DOOR
WHEN THE *WALL'S* CAVED IN

Weir reels back from the mike stand
the two drummers in hot pursuit

audience tripping its brains apart
a truly high moment!
you had to have been there
we've *all* been there
but where does the sound stop
—and where do we begin?
definitely extraspace thinking
and extraspace music
right to the final crescendo
the crowd's roar shivers the bones
well done! fucking *great* shit!

"ALTHEA"

oooooooooh, instant recognition
Garcia has a patent on this one
graceful leading notes
—*un*mistakable

I TOLD ALTHEA
I WAS FEELING LOST
LACKIN' IN SOME DIRECTION

*Now if Freud was on the right track,
and all human motivation basically
derives from the libido, or sexual
energy (with sex equaling sensual),
then live music and dance has
got to be the original group body-
consciousness movement and a
direct line to our primal energy
sources. Sensitive poet-singer-
songwriters forgive my metaphor,
but "in concert" may be the only way
that 9000 people can make love to
each other simultaneously.*

Darcie Sanders
Chicago Express, *November 8-14, 1973*

these guys are *on,* man
this band is *smokin'*
our hearts . . . overflowin'
Brent delicately laying in fills
imperturbable
patient and observant
Kreutzmann keeps it moving
stepping right in time

**LOOSE WITH THE TRUTH
MAYBE IT'S YOUR FIRE
BUT BABY, DON'T GET BURNED**

a study in miniature, you could say
gives us pause to consider
Grateful Dead 101
Jerry Garcia at the chalkboard
drawing the classic solo
a signature all his own
felt so deeply, so intensely
twisting and tugging at the melody
str-r-r-r-r-e-t-c-h-i-n-g it
like potter's clay
they say it was like this
when Louis Armstrong played

—back in the '20s
when Louis was a young man
his solos mesmerized the dancers
at times butter soft
then diamond hard
chorus after chorus
Garcia stands alone too
bending to the task
discerning pathways, relationships
different ways to look at things
suggesting the infinite
all the while, a delighted world

of friends out front
contemplating each new sculpture
a pleasure to give him our support
so there's a big hand at the end

"PASSENGER"

FIREFLY
CAN YOU SEE ME?

breathless
music with an appetite

SHINE ON, GLOWING
BRIEF AND BRIGHTLY

brisk, high drama
taut-bellied, with an edge
the band egging Weir on
a "Function at the Junction"
in the old Motown sense

UPSIDE OUT, OR INSIDE DOWN
FALSE ALARM
THE ONLY GAME IN TOWN

Cyn and Jane are eyeing Bobby
hmmmmmmmmmmmmm, *very nice!*
snickers and grins all around

A RAGIN' BEAST

such a heartbreaker

WITH NOTHING TO HIDE!

the wave breaks
the cataclysm dissolves
people stretch and purr

A Dead concert is my Sun Dance, and I eagerly await the festivities and rituals of cleansing and reintegrating my humanness. Each event retains its own special significance, and remains in my mind as moments of shamanistic ecstasy. The participation in each dance enables my spirit to transcend my body and mingle and rejoice and be one with the spirits of all the other participants.

Dead Head letter
Brentwood, California, 1973

"CHINA CAT SUNFLOWER"

we stomp our approval
a virtuoso display piece
a composition for showing off chops
ornate, yet refined
intellectually nourishing
—Grateful Dead chamber music!
my friend Alan laughs and laughs
Garcia's lead squalls like a tomcat
arching and crackling
on target, yet out of control
I feel like *I'm* out of control!
but I'm listening intently
as the Dead approach the bridge
the guitar interlude
the jangle
metal biting on metal
high-winding, racing-car synchromesh
perfectly interfaced precision parts
polished, greased, and oiled
stoked to the max

cohesion
beyond
belief
and then a subtle transmission shift
and we're over the hump
dropping into "I KNOW YOU RIDER"
solid thumping from both drummers
Brent so very resolute

GONNA MISS YOUR BABY
FROM ROLLING IN YOUR ARMS

good work, everybody!
the band glowing on stage
—the audience glowing within
oh, this feels sublime

I'D SHINE MY LIGHT THROUGH
THE COOL COLORADO RAIN

the reassuring verses
the uplifting solos

semi-a cappella into
clapping into
the all-time marvelous, prescient
transition into silence
everyone joining to make the spell
as the Dead's voices fill the air

I KNOW YOU RIDER
GONNA MISS ME WHEN I'M GONE

and in the end
respectful cheers

"JACK STRAW"

bright red light on Bobby
earnestly shouting, as always
a ragged Western tragedy
life as fragments and flashes
the music fading in and out
sometimes I'm there, sometimes not
but I manage to notice things

—like the T-shirt in front of me:
When There's No More
Room In Hell
The Dead Will Walk The Earth
but all my friends are grinning
and Weir is throwing back his head

JACK STRAW FROM WICHITA
CUT HIS BUDDY DOWN!

we admire Bob's fine strumming
what a pair of hands on that fella!
the " youthful, ebullient Robert Weir "
—Bill Graham said that once—
(remember the Felt Forum tape?)
but listen to Lesh's thunderclaps
the undercurrent pulse
he provides the necessary structure
for Bobby's Zane Grey ending
yes, very handsome work
on the part of everyone concerned

"TERRAPIN"

a song like towering redwoods
swaying majestically overhead

LET MY INSPIRATION FLOW
IN TOKEN RHYME
SUGGESTING RHYTHM

everyone seems frozen in time
even Dan Healy, captain of the board
deep in the audience
rocking back and forth, intent
captivated like any Dead Head
yes, there are vignettes all around
personal, individual triumphs
like Christmas lights
flashing on and off
you cannot but sway
caught in the wash of the music
tell me truly, is there a cure
for all this synaesthesia?

WHICH OF YOU TO GAIN ME, TELL
WILL RISK UNCERTAIN
PAINS OF HELL

in the thick soup of sound
it's so hard to absorb everything
especially with my imagination
playing in the rafters
it's Be Here Now
—a timeless experience
feeling like the very first time
forever perplexing
exposing every kind of nerve
my friends bob and weave around me
like shadowboxers in a puppet show
duck the shoulders! pound the hips!
this is grand, healthy tumult
our very own, individual theater

(TERRAPIN)
I CAN'T FIGURE OUT

It's hard to keep from smiling when you talk about the Dead.

(TERRAPIN)
IF IT'S THE END OR BEGINNING
(TERRAPIN)
BUT THE TRAIN'S
PUT ITS BRAKES ON
(TERRAPIN)
AND THE WHISTLE IS SCREAMING
TERRAPIN!

we enter now the forbidden chasm
a dense rain forest
monstrous vegetation shunted aside
by billowing thunder-chords
and snarling guitars
snaking through the undergrowth
we dance single file to the isthmus
people in the audience
arranging themselves in long rows
needing room to spill it all out
ebbing and flowing, never ceasing
a universal primal response

to this exhilarating dance music
concocted right before our eyes

into "PLAYING IN THE BAND"

glorious—and unexpected!
Weir is going nuts

SAY IT ONCE AGAIN NOW
WHOA
I HOPE YOU'LL UNDERSTAND

yes, message received
a familiar communique
this song is a trusty warhorse
eager for a new tilt in the lists
but it all sounds *fresh*
each passage wet cement
into which we press our hearts
a people's anthem
a song we know so well
newly minted

differently accented
changed in subtle ways
to reflect the here and now
yet it betokens the passage of time
the warp of distance and history
and we go round and round anew
in our Grateful Dead fishbowl
all of us swimming with the tide

YOU JUST KEEP A-TURNING
WHILE I'M *PLAYING* IN THE BAND

an echo of the roundabout theme
and down into a long jazzy section
your prototypic first set jam
disciplined, shipshape
all battened down
heading out to sea one more time
fisherman's choice, catch of the day

into "THE WHEEL"

Above and right: Grateful Dead play the Haight, San Francisco, March 3, 1968. Photos by Jim Marshall.

THE WHEEL IS TURNING
AND YOU CAN'T SLOW IT DOWN

a feeling of inside out

YOU CAN'T LET GO
AND YOU CAN'T HOLD ON

my perceptions so very altered

YOU CAN'T GO BACK
AND YOU CAN'T STAND STILL

why does everything feel so
astonishingly *odd*?

IF THE THUNDER DON'T GET YOU
THEN THE LIGHTNING WILL

it's elusive, resists pointed fingers
dances away
—becomes something else

EVERY TIME THAT WHEEL
TURN AROUND
BOUND TO COVER
JUST A LITTLE MORE GROUND

fact is,
it will drive you insane with
happiness
these are OK heroes
and I'm proud to be here
flowing right along
hippy-dipping to the music

into "THE MUSIC NEVER STOPPED"

great roar of pleasure

tapers must be going bananas
Lesh's bass pulls it all into shape
and Weir steps forward

THERE'S MOSQUITOES
ON THE RIVER
FISH ARE RISING UP LIKE BIRDS

a curious rhythm, genial, friendly
country homespun, easy on the ears
gradually transmogrified into jazz
not so tightly wound as "PLAYIN'"
and yet this too begins to change
into something wickedly arousing
our world carved away, dissolving
into expanded cinema of the brain
a brother/sisterhood of horror
paralyzing forces in total control

I've been to a lot of concerts, a whole lot of concerts. THOUSANDS of concerts. Concerts with new bands. Concerts with old favorites. Festivals with hundreds of thousands of people in the audience. But when those houselights went off, I heard something I've never heard in my life. It wasn't so much that the ovation was a loud ovation—it was very loud, to be sure—but it was this TONE. There was a sound in the yell the crowd gave that was unmistakable; the sound of pure unadulterated, unfettered LOVE, shameless and fierce, pouring out endlessly in one unbroken roar, and it was, no kidding, the most moving sound I have ever heard in my life. I will remember it till the day I die. Such affection!

And there we were, peaking on MDA, at my second Dead concert, with this ungodly roaring all around us, and up onstage, six guys plugging in, setting controls, tuning up, as if they were alone at a rehearsal, and Jerry Garcia was all gray. It had been ten years since I'd last seen him; there was no gradual transition for me. There he was, all of 38 years going on 50? 60?, his back to the audience, this roaring going on and on and on, and my vision shaking and skidding from MDA, and I had a vision of a very old Grateful Dead years from now, still carrying on, still truckin' away, an audience of adoring fans like this audience, still out there, and it was a thought both beautiful and scary at once. And then the band started to play.

Dead Head letter
1980

all eyes forward
meeting the tidal wave head on
a propelling
perforating feedback
psychopathic dissonance
burning screeches, blurs
cracking the bone marrow
awful, furious, and splendid
peaking
maybe the highest moment thus far
you can see it on all our faces
we felt the difference!
a community of understanding
good show!

"CASEY JONES"

a perfect capstone to this set

Mickey hammers away in glee
jackhammering, layin' that track,
loud loud loud in our ears
this is a no-bullshit song
it goes one way
and what a ride, my God

SWITCHMAN'S SLEEPING,
TRAIN 102
IS ON THE WRONG TRACK
AND HEADED FOR YOU

giant pistons of beat
careening 'round the bend
nothing
nothing can stop the iron horse now
nothing

DRIVIN' THAT TRAIN

inexorable
utterly implacable
faster, and faster still
till the final, chilling
clamorous conclusion
no more track

everyone is hoarse with relief
"We'll take a short break . . ."
and Weir heads for the wings
brother Jonas is hugging Jane
exhausted but completely happy
pleased and ridiculous
extremely silly
we collapse in a puddle of friends
must take stock of our situation
stoned to the gills, I'd say
and *so much more* to come! ∎

First Set **43**

Time is like a handful of sand. The tighter you grasp it, the faster it runs through your fingers. But if you caress it, it will leave in its wake memories of its gentle flow, rather than the roughness of its stones.
Dead Head letter
1981

Photo by Jim Marshall.

The Atlanta concert was the first time I ever let the music make love to me, caress my body and stroke my soul; the first time the music let me crawl into it and explore all its sides; dive in it, leap out of it, swim around in it; then use it as a catapult to a star-lit sky where electric neon angel-fish fly by night and the music marinates your mind till there is none of you left at all...and you're free to scamper the universe.

Dead Head letter
Atlanta, Georgia, 1977

Photo by Richard McCaffrey.

"You should open yourself up, empty yourself," says Anne from San Rafael, **"and let the music fill you from head to toe —as if it were water filling an empty vessel."**

Blair Jackson
BAM, *April 4, 1980*

My friend she say to me, "Day [that's me], the Grateful Dead they play wonderful music and Jerry Garcia will play to your heart and to your very soul."

And so, on a Friday the 13th, we leave Juneau behind as we board the ferryboat in my little truck and head for Anchorage. All the way I am getting instruction from Lynda who is who and who plays what, sings what and where and why. I drive more miles than I have in eight years (Juneau's "road" goes 50 miles and ends). We arrive in Anchorage and go to the high school auditorium where the shows will be and my friend she buys me tickets to all three shows and says, "Day, you will *love* it."

So, the very first night I stumble around looking at the people waiting to see the show. I watch them watching me watching them…I take it all in and take my seat. The musicians come out and they play for a little while.

The second night we are sitting in the balcony. The music sounds real fine from up there. My heart it is filling with joy and my God, look at all those drums. I love those drums…yes!

By the final show, I was taking pictures from the very front of the stage and Jerry looked up over those cute little sunglasses and smiled to me as I took his picture (no film of course—ran out ten pictures ago). I threw him a kiss for such a nice smile and went back to my seat. My heart I left on the edge of the stage. I went back for it later.

Dead Head letter
Juneau, Alaska, 1980

WEIR: "For some reason we've come up with a curious sort of chemistry that creates an energy bubble. The way we relate to the audience and the way they relate back to the band…"

HART: "And to each other…"

WEIR: "And to each other, so it creates an atmosphere…"

HART: "A good ambiance…"

WEIR: "…which is a great ambiance to be playing music in."

HART: "The situation is having a good time, and fun is part of the music, and if you have all these elements in one place, you're over. And that's why the Dead Heads keep coming back. They're making it. They're making a good time for themselves. They could make a bad time for themselves as well, but they've decided that this sort of thing makes them feel good."

Is that inspiring?

WEIR: "Hell yes! You can look forward to being one of the component parts of a genuine joyous event, and it takes audience participation to make it a genuine joyous event."

HART: "But it's also joyous in the future, as far as we're concerned. We see that going on, and there's hope for us. They see that going on, and it's hope for them. There's hope."

Chris Turkel
The (New York) News World, *January 12, 1979*

Photo by Ken Friedman ▶

Photo by Ken Friedman.

Photo by Ken Friedman.

Photo by Ken Friedman.

Photo by Ken Friedman.

Photo by Mary Ann Mayer.

Photo by Mary Ann Mayer.

Photo by John Werner.

Top, left to right: Phil Lesh, bass guitar; Bob Weir, guitar and vocals; Jerry Garcia, guitar and vocals; Brent Mydland, keyboards and vocals; Mickey Hart, drums and other percussion.

Bottom, left to right: Bill Kreutzmann, drums and other percussion; Donna Godchaux, vocals (from 1972 through 1979); backstage at the Warfield Theater in San Francisco with Tom Davis, of the comedy team Franken and Davis, and the Grateful Kids, October, 1980; the Dead at the Berkeley, California, Greek Theater, May, 1982.

Photo by Ed Perlstein.

Photo by Rick Brackett.

oto by Ken Friedman.

Top: Lesh and Garcia at El Camino Park in Palo Alto, California, June, 1967. Photo by Peter Tracy.

Above: Hawking Dead T-shirts at Colorado's Red Rocks Amphitheater.

Left: The Sky River Festival at Sultan, Washington, September 2, 1968. Photo by Jim Marshall.

Photo by Ken Friedman.

Gaelic Park, Bronx, New York, 1971. Photo by Chuck Pulin.

First Set **59**

I'm off again
in rapture and excitement
where the music of
"The Dead" takes my soul
to endless limits
in space, in time,
to the vast beauty where
wide open space prevails and
time is no matter
I feel the warmth and
the sensations that lift
my spirit.

Dead Head poem
Morgantown, West Virginia, 1981

"It's like a pact," says one Dead Head. "We show up and give the Dead our good energy, and they fill us up in return." Everyone erupts into self-conscious laughter. "It sounds kinda stupid when you talk about it."

Blair Jackson
BAM, *April 4, 1980*

Warfield Theater, San Francisco, October, 1980. Photo by Richard McCaffrey.

Donna Godchaux. Photo by Mary Ann Mayer.

Jerry Garcia:
"We try to start on a kind of easy-to-hear level—it works for several reasons that way. For one thing, it works that we remember how to play, each time, by starting with simple things, moving into more complex things, and then finally after having built a kind of platform, then we sort of jump off it.

"But if we were to start the show jumping off it, most of the audience I don't think would really be able to follow it, unless they were really Grateful Dead freaks. So we have this sort of continuum, which is good for us and it's good for the audience, a kind of continuity—from off the street to outer space, so to speak."

To Steve Peacock
Rock, 1972

Jerry Garcia:
"We have a certain amount of faith that the Grateful Dead is a special thing in ways that we aren't able to articulate. But we know it experientially, because it's an experience rather than a thought or an idea; it's something that's somehow fundamental to humanness, and whatever ritual and celebrations are all about."

To Lynn Van Matre
Chicago Tribune, *July 5, 1981*

Keith Godchaux. Photo by Ed Perlstein.

The three main points of the Dead Head worldview are the warm sharing of a family; the hippie contempt for commerciality that makes them stubbornly condescending to most other rock bands; and a noisy but peaceful determination to have a good time.

Dennis McNally
California Living, *September 28, 1980*

Brent Mydland. Photo by Chuck Pulin.

Bill Kreutzmann. Photo by Jim Marshall.

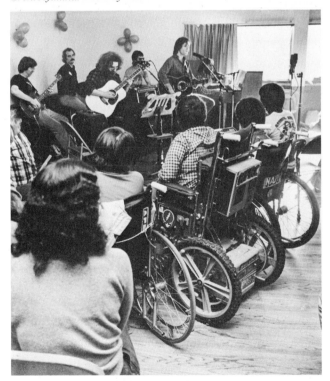

Grateful Dead concert at the Mill Valley, California, Recreation Center,
December 6, 1980. Photo by Ray Baltar.

Jerry Garcia. Photo by Jon Sievert.

The Dead and the New York Dead Heads in Central Park, May 5, 1968. Photos by Ken Greenberg.

Air guitar at Lille, France, May 13, 1972. Photo by Mary Ann Mayer.

Follow the south wind, traditionally benign but loaded today with cold rain and solid clouds, driving a heavy sky across the south of England, aiming with singleminded malice for Bickershaw, near Wigan in Lancashire, scouring round and round the oval, maybe three-quarters of a mile the long way, where the Bickershaw Festival is freezing to death late in the afternoon of Sunday, May 7th. A lot of rain and many pairs of feet have churned the soil to a harsh, thick mud—not at all the fun glop featured at other festivals. You could play in this stuff, but you get the feeling ancient skulls and kneecaps are just below the surface.

The performers have to face not only the chilled and ex-hausted crowd but the wind itself. Throughout the morning and early afternoon it drives in under the roof of the stage, right in the faces and against the numb fingers of the musi-cians. The wind seems determined that no one will get it on today. And so the Dead take their time setting up. A big space heater shows up stage left, one of those tank-on-wheels jobs that blasts out a fan of superheated air that nor-mally warms up places like drafty aircraft hangars. But it can't really be helping all that much; it might keep the fin-gers just this side of blue.

"Truckin'" starts the set, and Weir's rhythm line reaches

out; the bass moves in underneath, loping along steadily. But it takes "Mr. Charlie" to really jolt the sand from the far corners of the eyes. Half the audience is really up for the first time, all alert, and the Dead freaks are grinning at each other through the afternoon dusk because they can see it developing, thousands of uninitiated finding out what a miserable Sunday can be good for. Then there's "Beat It On Down the Line," the one that always seems faster than it is, or is faster than it seems, probably Lesh knows which. He remains intent and calm as ever, playing with concentration and only an occasional, weirdly choirboy smile flashed to the others. We're told it's Bill's birthday, which may explain why he and Pigpen, mostly serious on stage, get off a couple of maniac grins to each other when Pig comes up to sing "You Lied, You Cheated," mellow and unforgiving and self-assured as only he can be.

Near the end of the first set, the Dead do "Playing in the Band," maybe too risky by the standards of a couple of hours ago, but only time can tell whether an audience can find the release and the hidden cataclysmic stomp in a long-ish jam. They can, because although the sun is down, the wind seems to have faded with it and the evening is very much on. Several songs back you noticed that nearly every-

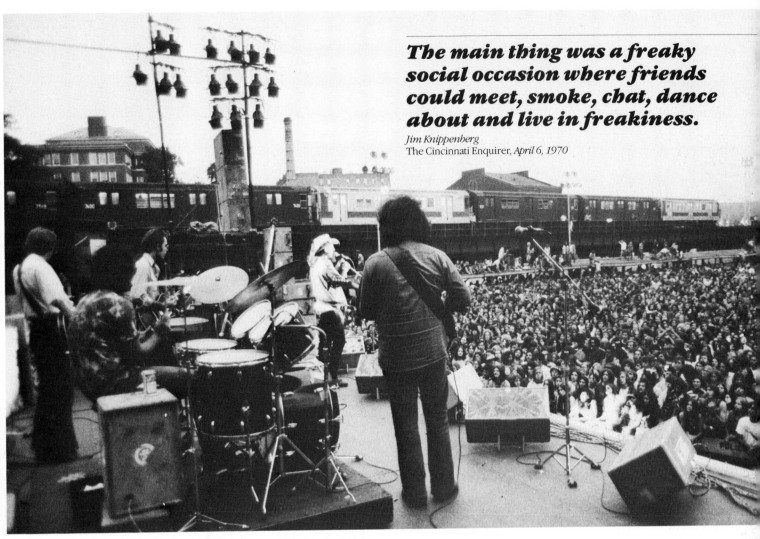

Gaelic Park, Bronx, New York, August 26, 1971. Photo by Chuck Pulin.

one is standing, clapping, dancing. And "Tennessee Jed" says, as "Mr. Charlie" did earlier, that a gradual loosening-up is in progress—so much so that these musical workmen can come in with pneumatic guitars and pound you into a pleasant state of brain damage. And here they come indeed, a long and raucous "Good Lovin'," that blasts back stronger with each chorus. The roar at its end could end this welcome, surprising set very nicely, but it's "Casey Jones" and a louder roar, choogling off down the track, sure to be back with a second set sooner than you think.

In purely visual terms, the scene calls up a Jim Morrison hellscape or the siege of Gondor, but there's too much pleasure in the air for that. Not even the Dead freaks can explain why this night, still cold, nowhere near dry, has so much energy. The glow from the stage and the bonfires is like the pagan philosophers' aura in Limbo, holding the dark at bay. Underneath, simple physical joy in the music. How it has gotten into the muscles and warmed them. It feels like an enormous campfire outing, 30,000 people more or less in line for the first time this weekend, ready to dance the embers down.

Dead Head letter
Millinocket, Maine, 1972

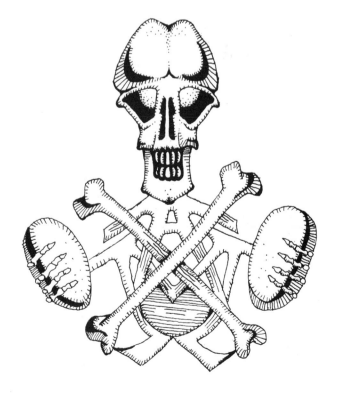

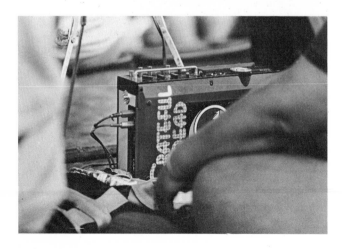

well, hi there man...

you don't know me but i got your list from a friend who
knows this person who is into dogs and he was taking his
norwegian elkhound out to take a shit and needed something to scrape up the shit off this old lady next door's lawn
and he just picked up some paper his roommate had laying
around and the paper turned out to be the list of yours. he
gave me the list, but there's so much shit on it that i can't
read it very good. but i saw your address so i wrote you
cause i want to trade tapes.

like gee, man, like wow what a fanfuckintastic list you
have man. wow like i thought MY list was impressive until i
saw your list. i would send you my list but i left it in my pants
pocket with my 10,000 hits of orange sunshine and my ma
washed the pants and the orange sunshine got all over my

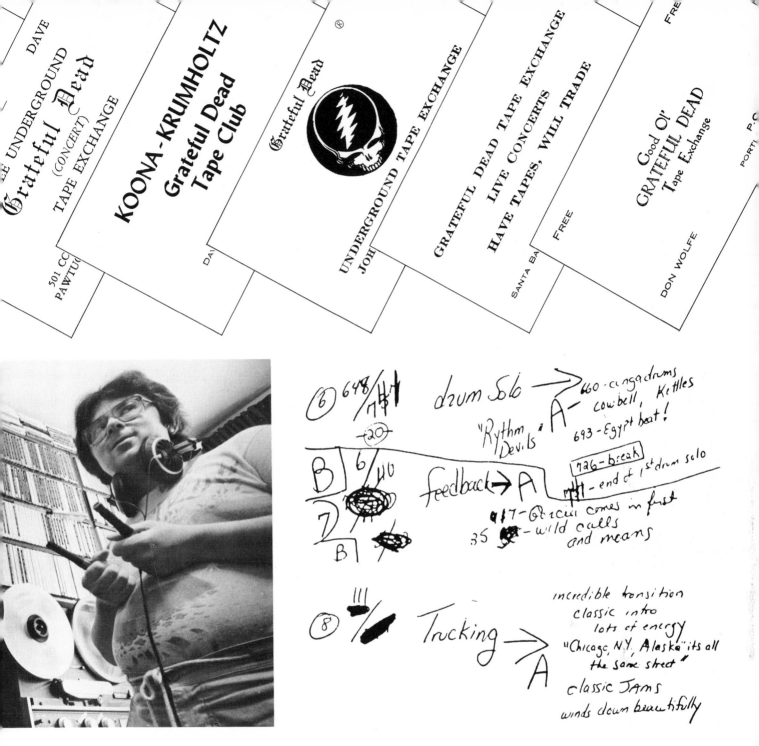

list so i had to eat the list to get high. anyway, my list is *real* extensive and i don't have a typewriter so its hard for me to write it all down. so i tell you what, why don't you just ask me for stuff and i'll see if i got it? sounds good, eh?

i have some terrrrrrrrriiiiiiffffffiiiiiiicccccccc stuff i KNOW you'll want like real fast, man. here are just a couple of examples…

i have a *great* 25 seconds of lesh belching before the second set at saskatchewan technological institute for retarded nurses. it'll just blow you away.

i've taken the shows i have of 1976 and simul-synced the second sets on top of the first sets to save space. far fuckin out, man.

and this'll really get you. i have the first chord of every show they played in 1979—all on one tape.

i never label any of my tapes. that's just wasting time. so i can send you a bunch of tapes and you can figure out what shows they are. i'm proud to say i do recording myself; i have a pocket groopipuki. it's only three inches long, and i use these neat little norelco dictating cassettes in it. really fools those security idiots.

since i know you're just dying to trade with me man, like i'll be sending you 147 maxells—just to start things off slow. make me your whole collection. i need it by the end of the month.

PS—the tapes will be coming C.O.D. in *big* boxes. i figured you could use some big boxes.

Dead Head letter
Hawaii, 1980

Jerry Garcia:
"I think that even our younger fans are the same kind of people as the last generation of Dead Heads. They're the seekers, the people who think there's more to it all than the regular rap."

To Matt Damsker
The (Philadelphia) Bulletin
November 24, 1978

Equipment-crew members Steve Parish (left) and Bill Candelario, 1972. Photo by Mary Ann Mayer.

Golden Gate Park, 1975. Photo by San Francisco Chronicle.

First Set **71**

It was one of those concerts where the Dead pulled out the Vista Cruiser not once, not twice, but for the entire damn show.

Letter to the editor
Dead Relix, *March-April, 1976*

Intermission

Everything's coming up skulls and roses.

I am taking the time
right now
to express my feelings.
You all have delighted
my mind and soul
for many years
and it's now
my turn
to let you know
that I've dug every moment
we've spent together
whether at a music hall
or
while I'm walking
the path of my life.
I feel as if I'm also
a part
of the Grateful Dead.
You
have helped me
spread the word.
*Dead Head poem
1980*

Roosevelt Stadium, Jersey City, New Jersey, 1972.

Marcia Steinburger and her best friend, Starglow Peterson, had hitchhiked into Mill Valley from Sacramento in the early afternoon and were now sitting in Sheila Titterwell's front room on the hillside of Mount Tam. Sheila lived with some guy neither Marcia nor Starglow knew, but about whom they had heard nice things. He was at work now and would be home shortly. In the meantime, the three young lovelies were smoking some very potent dope, and were sitting on Sheila's floor watching the orange sun go down. By dusk, they were all four joints to the cosmos, and everything was a barrel of laughs.

"And that crazy fart is going to be home any minute," Sheila laughed as she took the toilet paper roll from Starglow. "You know what he does now? He comes screaming up that hill each night with Hugh Jardon, hollering as loud as he can like an asshole, 'GET OUT THE PIPE, PUT ON THE DEAD, AND SPREAD!' And like the cat is stark raving naked by the time he hits the front door." Sheila laughed again and shook her head, and then inhaled deeply on the roll.

"Put on the dead, and spread?" Marcia looked puzzled. Sheila raised one slim finger, held her breath a few seconds longer, and then exhaled slowly.

"Right. As in the Grateful Dead and legs. Real George thinks that it's the greatest to…"

She was interrupted as the quiet of the early evening disintegrated around them in a confusion of sound and squalor as the high whine of a VW wound down to a quick halt, and a huge voice called up to them.

"PUT ON THE DEAD AND SPREAD, 'CAUSE I'M LOADED AND READY TO GO!"

"It's Real George now," Sheila said jumping to her feet. "Excuse me." She pulled her sweater up over her head and off her arms, and then slipped out of her jeans. She was naked in a jiffy. "It's been like this for a week now."

She quickly crossed the room to the tape deck, threaded a reel, and turned the machine on.

The two visiting girls peered at her for a long moment, and then turned their attention to the strange shadow figure charging up the front steps and leaving a trail of clothes strewn wildly behind him. He was going like sixty.

"Ever since he got that album," Sheila said as she opened the bedroom door, "Real George likes nothing better than to fuck to the Grateful Dead. It makes him on fire." She winked. "It's groovy." Sheila then disappeared in the darkness of the bedroom.

And just as the Dead began "Dark Star," Real George hit the front door with his naked pink and hairy body and crashed through into the living room.

"Da da!"

Marcia's and Starglow's mouths fell open as the fleeting vision swept through the room for a brief moment before disappearing along with Sheila in the darkness.

"Ahhh," someone said in there as Marcia and Starglow exchanged quizzical glances. "Ahh." The music grew louder.

"That's far out," Starglow said.

"Very far out," Marcia nodded.

The two girls turned around and looked back out into the hills. Already lights were beginning to come on as the land grew blacker.

"Gee, I wish I had a date tonight," Marcia finally said.

J.R. Young
Rolling Stone, *February 7, 1970*

Guitar PLAYER

OCTOBER 1978
$1.25

Jerry Garcia
FOUNDER OF THE GRATEFUL DEAD

PLUS...
John Tropea
Liona Boyd
Al Caiola
Jazz Guitar Duos

Fifty Great Books for Christm...

NEW WEST

New Life for the Grateful Dead
By Charlie Haas

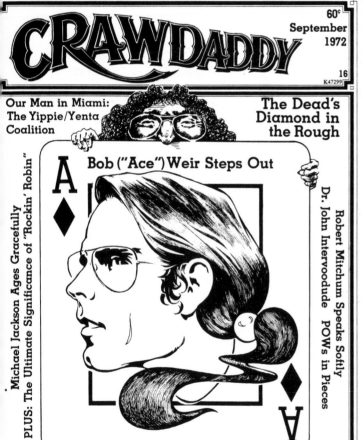

60¢
September 1972
16
K47299

CRAWDADDY

Our Man in Miami:
The Yippie/Yenta
Coalition

The Dead's
Diamond in
the Rough

Bob ("Ace") Weir Steps Out

Michael Jackson Ages Gracefully
PLUS: The Ultimate Significance of "Rockin' Robin"

Robert Mitchum Speaks Softly
Dr. John Intervoodude
POWs in Pieces

A Kind Word for Joan Baez

zigzag35
pence
vol3 .no11

THE GRATEFUL DEAD

DON NIX
COMMANDER CODY
GRAM PARSONS

UN-RELEASED GENESIS TRACK FREE INSIDE

ern Forests

Section:

DEA

e memory
neakiest
Tricky Dicky

Personalities and Band Secrets

Phil   reads extremely fast … energetic! … played bass only as long as he's been in the band … quick mind … doesn't bleach his hair …

Bill   sleeps a lot … eats a lot … digs jazz drummers … has a shiny new Mustang … not quiet at all … business minded … used to sell wigs … giggles a lot …

Jer   talented, talented … has a lot to say … digs girls, girls … very open … loves orange juice … tells the best stories … warm … hates dishonesty (they all do) … owns a pedal steel guitar … Leo …

Pig   rides a BSA … walks around the house in strange outfits … has a bright red bathrobe … sings Blue Danube in the shower … washes his hair a lot … afraid of bees, but he's not afraid of mice … kind … plays blues on the guitar boss …

Bob   on Zen macrobiotic diet … super nice guy … got A's in school … got kicked out of seven … nickname Mr. Bob Weir Trouble …

From The Olompali Sunday Times, *the first Grateful Dead newsletter, 1967.*

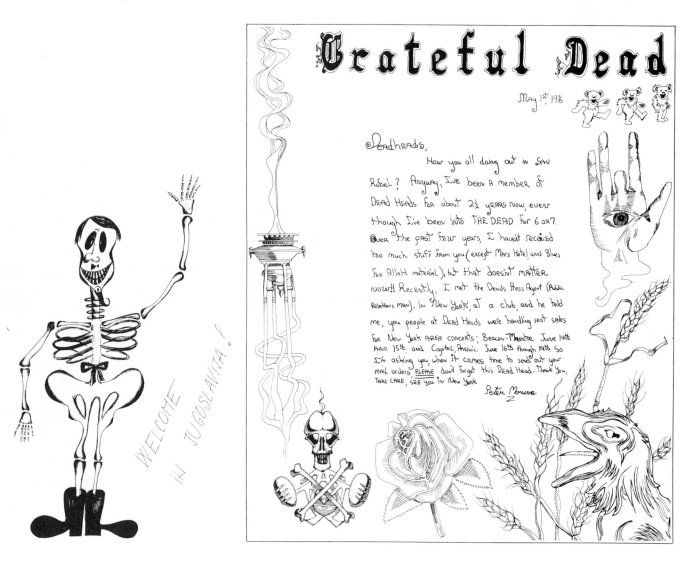

Grateful Dead

May 1st 1976

Deadheads,

How you all doing out in San Rafael? Anyway, I've been a member of Dead Heads for about 2½ years now, even though I've been into The Dead for 6 or 7. Over the past few years, I haven't received too much stuff from you (except Mars Hotel, and Blues For Allah material), but that doesn't matter now!! Recently, I met the Deads Press Agent (Public Relations man), in New York, at a club, and he told me, you people at Dead Heads were handling seat sales for New York Area concerts; Beacon-Theatre June 14th and 15th and Capitol, Passaic June 16th through 19th So I'm asking you, when it comes time to send out your Mail orders, PLEASE don't forget this Dead Head. Thank You, Take Care, See you in New York

Peter Morena

WELCOME IN JUGOSLAVIA!

These are a few of our family from Cheif Mt. up in the hills of Frisco, Colo. (A small turkey town that's growing like a fungus!)

Me   Johnathan Steven Fred   Chris Fred   Rick Mike Dan   Paul Pat Jeff Gene &
              (my brother)   (the red)   (Ricks brother)   (My other Anne
                                                                              brother)

THANK You!!

(for a real good time)

DEAD HEADS
SAN RAFAEL

22.06.1974 year

Galati
29.01.1981.

Dear friends,

You are for me the best formation of rock and roll, and your pieces, nice songs, for meditation, make me happy, my soul is not close and receive your minds!

I think that yours fillings are taking in your music and ever your music will remain like Beethoven's or Schumann's, Verdi's music!

But, this letter is too small for write all the words in my mind. Not so much as ten pages don't suffice to write so much!

Now, I want request some desires!

Please mail me a signed picture, or a poster for my room. Must to tell you that I collect all the pictures with yours portraits, and yours stories!

I espect your answer and I wish many successes in yours activities!

Thank you anticipate

Yours sincerelly
Thank you again!

My address is:
CRISTEA TACHE
8200 GALATI
Str. Elicei, 11
ROMANIA –

P.S. Excuse me for the wrong in English!
Please, enclose the envelope! Thank you!

Dear Dead Heads!

I live in Poland. I'm 24 years old man. In last year I'm finished study in Torun University. A few years ago I was interesting in music of Vanilla Fudge. After Vanilla Fudge decomposition I listened music from West Coast of U.S.A. – first of all Grateful Dead.

I suppose in this while Grateful Dead is best band in the world. Their music is for me peculiary suggestive, authentic and besides – excellent from musical side.

I please Yours send me exact informations about past, present and future time of Grateful Dead.

I send for Dead Heads many best, brotherly greetings
– Krzysztof

My adress:
KRZYSZTOF CHOJNACKI
ul. NIEDZIAŁKOWSKIEGO 29
14-240 SUSZ
POLAND

May 26, 1976

Dear Deadheads —

Wow! Us older gals & guys really were neglected — we weren't given the "opportunity" to catch the Dead — and we don't want to see the Egyptian Grateful Dead yet.

Our noses were permanently knocked out of joint — sorely disappointed — not "satisfied & tickled too" — You used to have us on your mailing list — eons ago when Deadheads were first established. Why? We have moved 4 times in the last 6 years. You know — KEEP ON TRUCKING and all that jazz. How can you ask present "Deadheads" to point the way to the future" when folks like us pointed it out to them long

Happy thoughts keep the heart in

ago. We helped make Dead what they still are today — a high level group — and they helped us as well. I remember the following "small theatre" N.Y. gigs — a) Palm Gardens b) the Dead (2nd billing) to Joplin & to Country Joe c) all the Fillmore gigs d) the benefit at the Anderson e) Central Park with Butterfield f) the Pavillion in Queens — We had the faith of them returning to small format and now we can't see them in our prefered environment.

They always were a dynamic group ... We that remember — we who once belonged to a small obscure "once & future cult of the Dead" now can't even get tickets to a small theatre — the way the tradition used to be — we refuse to go as lemmings to a large stadium.

Oh, the lacerations of life —

Ms. Roni Anne Piastuch
Charles Lohr Poresky

WARNER BROS. RECORDS
WB
PROMOTION NOT FOR SALE
★   ★

GRATEFUL DEAD
Produced by
Bob Weir,
Phil Lesh,
and
Betty Cantor

WB 7667
(QAA5607)
3:57
Intro: :13
From the Warner
Bros. Album
3WX 2668
"EUROPE '72"

SUGAR MAGNOLIA
(Weir-Hunter)
Ice Nine Pub. Co. - ASCAP
℗1972 Warner
Bros. Records Inc.

WARNER BROS. RECORDS INC. A SUBSIDIARY AND LICENSEE OF WARNER BROS., INC.   MADE IN U.S.A.

SH
RECORD

ALABAMA GETAWAY
(Garcia-Hunter)
GRATEFUL DEAD
PRODUCED BY GARY LYONS
UNAUTHORIZED DUPLICATION IS A
VIOLATION OF APPLICABLE LAWS
Arista Records, Inc. Arista Bldg., 6 West 57th Street, New York, NY 10019

SIRS:

I have this stereo, see, an old one, portable, and I lent it to these cats and they broke the changer arm, so now whenever I want to put a stack of records on, I have to place them one at a time on the spindle and balance them there. Well, this has been going on for a couple of months now, and there is one thing that I have noticed: the only records that stay perfectly balanced on the spindle are my Dead records; all the others either lean over to the right or lean over so far that they touch the record playing. What do you think of that?! Probably the same thing I do.

Chris Tomkins
Charlottesville, VA

Letter to the editor
Rolling Stone, *July 23, 1970*

"It always appeared to me, being responsible for the sale of their records, like trying to push an elephant through a keyhole," said Ron Rakow, president of Grateful Dead Records in the '70s. "Their breadth and depth cannot be contained on the dimension of a piece of black plastic. It just can't happen."

Betty Ann Powell
The Santa Fe (New Mexico) Reporter, *February 26, 1981*

Photo by Robert Vernon Wilson © Natural Photography 1982.

WARNER BROS.- SEVEN ARTS RECORDS
PROMOTION [W] NOT FOR SALE

THE GRATEFUL DEAD

7324
(M 17135)

Arranged by
The Grateful
Dead
From The
Warner Bros.-
Seven Arts
Album WS 1790
"AOXOMOXOA"

COSMIC CHARLIE
(Hunter-Garcia-Lesh)
Ice Nine Publishing Co.
BMI - 5:40

MADE IN U.S.A. WARNER BROS.-SEVEN ARTS RECORDS, INC. A SUBSIDIARY AND LICENSEE OF WARNER BROS.-SEVEN ARTS, INC.

GRATEFUL DEAD

S. BLUES 3:12
(Hunter-Garcia)
ce Nine (ASCAP)

STEREO
SIDE A

JOHNNY B. GOODE
(Chuck Berry)
Arc Music Corp. - BMI

MADE IN U.S.A.

BROS. RECORDS, INC. A SUBSIDIARY AND LICENSEE OF WARNER BROS., INC.

TRUCKIN'

Bob Weir:
"Once you present a song from on stage, that's pretty much where it comes together. We should make a blanket policy of not recording anything that we haven't played on stage. One of the reasons we don't make good records, generally, is because we don't know the material when we're doing it—we don't *know* the material until years later. A record is an idealized version."

To David Gans
1981

87

Alaska Getaway

Paul Grushkin at Sunshine's Dead wall, San Francisco, 1980.   Photo by Ed Perlstein.   ®

I took a taxi from the airfield to the edge of town. From there, I traveled to Beverly Hoffman's house in a boat. It was a wooden shack, built up on pilings, on the riverbank, twenty feet above the normal level of the water. The boat dropped me at the front door.

Beverly Hoffman was twenty-five years old and 25 percent Eskimo. She lived in the house with John McDonald, a tall, quiet man with a red beard, with whom she had formerly lived in San Francisco, and by whom she was now pregnant. Their friend Tom Foote, from San Francisco, also lived there. His girlfriend had recently moved to a different house, a few blocks away, due to personal differences with Tom Foote.

There were more than two hundred Hoffmans in Bethel, including the mayor of the town, the owner of the fuel company, and Beverly's father, who ran the biggest shipping company in western Alaska. One uncle, the president of the local Native association, had traveled to the White House a few years earlier and had presented a box of dried fish to President Ford. Beverly had five brothers and two sisters,

and so many first cousins that there were some she did not recognize when she passed them on the street.

She had gone to high school in Anchorage. It had been expected that she would then return to Bethel. Instead, over her father's strenuous objections, she went to Palm Beach Junior College in Florida. "I needed to find out who I was," she said. "At home, I was just a baby-sitter and a maid."

In Florida, for the first time, she became involved with marijuana, with the peace movement, and with men. After two years, she moved to El Paso, Texas, to live near a friend who was stationed at an army base there. Soon she wound up in San Francisco, where she met John McDonald, who had recently been discharged from the Army after a tour of duty that had involved electronic reconnaissance in Vietnam. They moved into a house on Frederick Street, living with a dozen other people. Tom Foote soon joined them there. He had been hitchhiking through Florida, vaguely planning to go to Australia someday, and had been picked up by a friend of Beverly's who was on her way to San Francisco for a visit. Tom Foote had come with her, and they eventually got married and moved to a farm in Illinois. The marriage failed, however, and Tom Foote returned to San Francisco by himself.

The group earned money by painting and renovating Victorian houses. There were ten bedrooms in the Frederick Street house and all of them were always full. The residents tried to pattern their lives after the philosophy of the rock group the Grateful Dead.

"Basically," said John McDonald, "as we perceived it, this meant doing things you really enjoyed with people you liked." They held frequent garage sales to raise money for tickets to Grateful Dead concerts. Once, everyone in the house saw the Grateful Dead perform for five nights in a row. In addition, Grateful Dead records and tapes were played in the house almost twenty-four hours a day.

After two years of this, Beverly and John, and Tom and his girlfriend, and one other couple, decided to go to Alaska for the summer. Their plan was to utilize Beverly's status as an Eskimo to obtain land under provisions of the Alaska Native Claims Settlement Act. A dentist from Bethel, who was hitchhiking back to Alaska following a vacation in Mexico, stopped off to see Beverly in San Francisco. He told them that if they reached Seattle by the middle of May, they might get a ride up on Ole Sumstad's barge, which was preparing for its annual trip.

They arrived, the six of them: Beverly, who was well known in the town, and her five non-Eskimo friends, who became instantly notorious as the first hippies ever to visit Bethel.

"Those first few weeks," Beverly said, "it seemed like we were all anybody could talk about. 'Hey, have you seen the hippies who came in with Bev Hoffman on the *Husky*?'"

Her father had not even wanted her to leave for college. He wanted even less for her to have returned in the sort of company she had chosen. He told everyone in Bethel not to give them jobs if they should ask, and he told Beverly, the first time he saw her, that he would make certain that they would never be able to find a place to live.

All summer long, they stayed in a tent on the riverbank, three miles from town. It rained every day for the first three weeks. They had no food, except what they fished from the river. During the day they were devoured by mosquitoes. At night they lived in fear that a vigilante group would attack. The third couple left quickly, on a Wien flight. But Beverly and John and Tom and his girlfriend remained. They were still in their tent as summer ended. Beverly told her father they would stay there through the winter if need be. She had come home, she told him, at the age of twenty-five, and it was none of his business who had accompanied her. Besides, she said, if he would just calm down long enough to get to know them, he would discover that her friends were not hippies at all, but energetic and intelligent individuals who, despite their fondness for long hair and old clothes and rock music and marijuana, wanted to make a commitment to Alaska.

Through the first snowfall, Beverly's father held firm. But when the river froze up, he relented to an extent. He still would not help them find jobs, but he did let them know that there was an old house available at the edge of the river downtown. He was, of course, convinced that winter would drive the "hippies" away. But figured he would just as soon

see it happen without also seeing his daughter freeze to death.

Beverly's father, however, had miscalculated. John and Tom and his girlfriend did not depart. For, already, they had discovered the one great truth about Bethel, the hidden attribute that more than compensated for the otherwise intolerable things about the place: in Bethel, if you had any resources at all, you could live out almost any fantasy you'd ever had.

Tom Foote, for example, had always liked books. Within six months—his lack of academic background notwithstanding—he was hired as the Bethel librarian, and was discovering federal grant programs that enabled him to order hundreds of new titles every month. Giving Bethel one of the finest libraries, for a community of its size, anywhere in America.

John McDonald had brought all of his Grateful Dead records north. In San Francisco, when he played them, he sometimes imagined he was producing his own radio show. In Bethel, within six months, he got a job as the morning disc jockey on a real radio station, beaming four hours of Grateful Dead out across the tundra every day. Except for the educational jingles on "Sesame Street," the Grateful Dead were just about the only music the Eskimos of western Alaska got to hear. In addition, because he owned a few good cameras, John McDonald became staff photographer for Bethel's weekly newspaper. He was planning, next year,

---

Except for "Sesame Street," the Grateful Dead were just about the only music the Eskimos of western Alaska got to hear.

---

to make a film of the sled dog race between Anchorage and Nome, and to develop a dog team himself. All of which seemed a considerably more interesting way to spend his life than repainting old houses in San Francisco.

Beverly Hoffman, as a Native, was appointed curator of Eskimo artifacts at the Kuskokwim Community College regional museum. She occasionally filled in on the morning radio show, slipping a little Jimmy Buffet in between tracks of the Dead. Having made peace with her father, she was planning to operate a forklift for his shipping company in the summer, for as long as her pregnancy would permit.

Tom Foote's girlfriend was helping to administer a federally funded program to aid children with learning disabilities. In San Francisco, she had not even been able to find work as a substitute teacher.

"It's amazing," said John McDonald. "It's almost like we staged a coup. Where else could you come to by barge, sleep in a tent, and six months later be controlling the media and reshaping the culture of the town?"

"The thing is," said Tom Foote, "in Bethel, whatever particular talent or ambition you may have, you can be pretty sure that you're the only person in town who has it."

Joe McGinniss
Going to Extremes, *1981*

An Experiment in Dream Telepathy with the Grateful Dead

Method

For the six-night study, an attempt was made to use a large number of telepathic agents in a situation which would involve some of the emotional intensity which characterizes spontaneous instances of telepathic transmission. The entire audience attending concerts by The Grateful Dead, a rock-and-roll musical group, was instructed to telepathically transmit an art print which was randomly selected just before it was projected on a screen above the musical group while they were performing.

Setting

The six concerts involved in this experiment were held at the Capitol Theater in Port Chester, N.Y., approximately 45 miles from the Dream Laboratory at Maimonides Medical Center in Brooklyn.

Subjects

Two "psychic sensitives," Malcolm Bessent and Felicia Parise, served as subjects for this study. Both had participated in previous studies of extrasensory effects at the Dream Laboratory (e.g., Krippner, 1970).

Mr. Bessent's dreams were monitored by standard psychophysiological techniques at the laboratory. Miss Parise slept at her apartment; she was telephoned from time to time during the night and asked for dream recall. Further, the audience at the Capitol Theater was told about Mr. Bessent's participation in the experiment but was not informed as to Miss Parise.

Procedure

Each of the six concerts was attended by about 2,000 persons. Further, it was apparent to observers at the concert that the majority of the people in the audience were in states of consciousness that had been dramatically altered by the time the art print was presented. These altered states of consciousness were brought about by the music, by the ingestion of psychedelic drugs before the concerts started, and by contact with other members of the audience. At 11:30 P.M., the following six-slide sequence was projected on a large screen:

1. YOU ARE ABOUT TO PARTICIPATE IN AN ESP EXPERIMENT.
2. IN A FEW SECONDS YOU WILL SEE A PICTURE.
3. TRY USING YOUR ESP TO "SEND" THIS PICTURE TO MALCOLM BESSENT.
4. HE WILL TRY TO DREAM ABOUT THE PICTURE. TRY TO "SEND" IT TO HIM.
5. MALCOLM BESSENT IS NOW AT THE MAIMONIDES DREAM LABORATORY IN BROOKLYN.
6. At this point, a randomly selected art print was projected on the screen.

The Grateful Dead continued to play while the slides were projected. Between numbers, they occasionally made comments regarding the experiment and the slides, thus drawing the audience's attention specifically to the material. The art print was projected for 15 minutes. As there was no "light show" on any of the six nights, the experimental material served as the only projected visual stimulus during the concert.

Evaluation

Evaluation was accomplished by giving two judges (M.B. and D.P.) all six dream-report transcripts for each subject as well as all six art prints actually used. The judges worked independently and had no contacts with each other, with the subjects, or with the staff members who had been at the laboratory on the nights of the experiments.

Each judge read the subject's transcripts and looked at the art prints. On a 100-point scale, he made a mark describing the degree of correspondence between the dreams and the art prints.

For Miss Parise, one correct pair obtained the highest rating. In the case of Mr. Bessent, the judges gave the highest scores to the correct pairs four times out of six. This distribution produces a critical ratio of 2.449 which is statistically significant at the .0124 level in a two-tailed test. Thus, for Mr. Bessent, the ESP hypothesis is supported.

Examples

On the night of February 19, 1971, "The Seven Spinal Chakras," by Scralian, was randomly selected as the target picture. This painting shows a man in the lotus position practicing yogic meditation. All seven "chakras" (energy centers of the body, centering around the spinal column) are vividly colored. Excerpts from Mr. Bessent's dreams follow:

I was very interested in…using natural energy.…I was talking to this guy who said he'd invented a way of using solar energy and he showed me this box…to catch the light from the sun which was all we needed to generate and store the energy…I was discussing with this other guy a number of other areas of communication and we were exchanging ideas on the whole thing.…He was suspended in mid-air or something.…I was thinking about rocketships …I'm remembering a dream I had…about an energy box and…a spinal column.

Conclusion

One of the two subjects in this experiment produced results which were statistically significant and which demonstrated his ability to receive impressions of a randomly selected target picture 45 miles distant. The experimental situation was tightly controlled; thus, extrasensory perception is the most likely explanation of the results.

Stanley Krippner, Ph.D., Charles Honorton, Montague Ullman, M.D.
The Journal of the American Society of Psychosomatic Dentistry and Medicine, *Volume 20, Number One, 1973*

"For Donna Godchaux" by an unknown artist.

WHAT A LO
STRANGE T
ITS BEE
1966 - 19

The Grateful Dead

STEAL YOUR FACE

LSC Presents The Grateful Dead in concert May 7 1970
MIT Armory 8:00 pm $3.00, $3.50 at the door

© KELLEY/G. DEAD 1978

1978

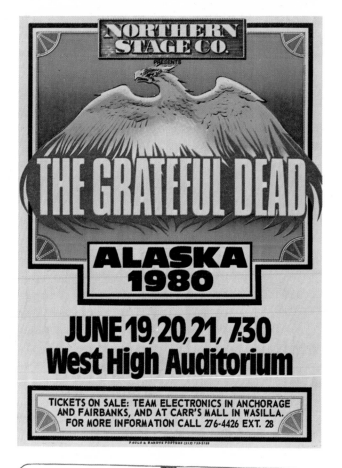

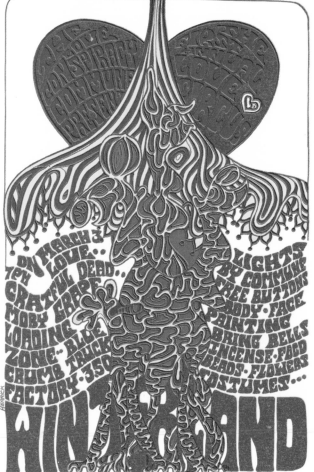

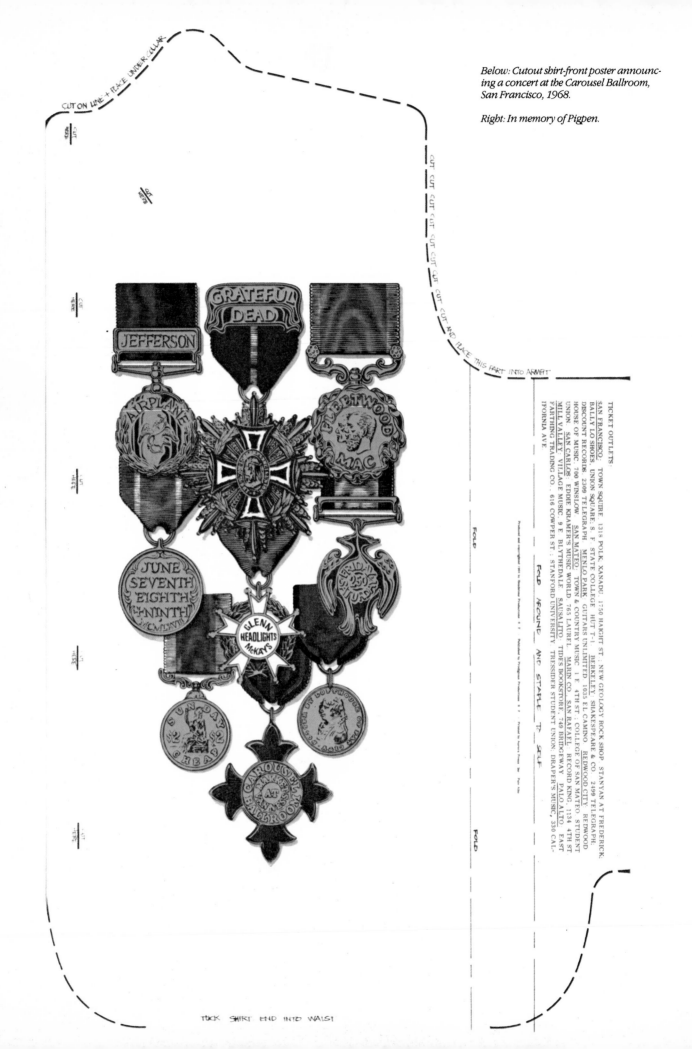

Below: Cutout shirt-front poster announcing a concert at the Carousel Ballroom, San Francisco, 1968.

Right: In memory of Pigpen.

FUNK & WAGNALLS

NEW PRACTICAL

Standard

[Reg. U. S. Pat. Off.]

DICTIONARY

OF THE ENGLISH LANGUAGE

EM'·PHA·TYPE *Method of Pronunciation*

CHARLES EARLE FUNK

Editor

BRITANNICA WORLD LANG

VOLUME ONE

...) ⸱ of 2GREET.

.ATE *verb* [GRA⸱ ⸱ ⸱GRAT·ING] 1 To rub to⸱ to produce a harsh, unpleasant sound. 2 To we⸱ minute particles by rubbing with some rough boa, strument. 3 To cause mental irritation; offend. [<Or. *grater* <LL. *crato*, scratch] — GRAT·ER *noun*.

2GRATE *noun* 1 A framework of bars, as to close an open-ing, or to hold fuel in burning. 2 A perforated metallic plate through which the ores pass after being crushed un-der stamps. 3 A fireplace. 4 [Obs.] A cage furnished with grates; a place of confinement.
— *tr. verb* [GRAT·ED, GRAT·ING] To fit with a grate or with bars. [<L. *cratis*, hurdle]

GRATE·FUL *adj.* 1 Having a due sense of benefits received; thankful. 2 Affording gratification; pleasurable; agreeable. 3 Expressing or denoting thankfulness; indicative of grati-tude. [<L. *gratus*, pleasing]
Synonyms: obliged, thankful. See AGREEABLE, DELIGHTFUL.
— ·LY *adv.* — ·NESS *noun*.

GRATEFUL DEAD The motif of a cycle of folk tales which begin with the hero's coming upon a group of people ill-treating or refusing to bury the corpse of a man who had died without paying his debts. He gives his last penny, either to pay the man's debts or to give him decent burial. Within a few hours he meets with a travelling companion who aids him in some impossible task, gets him a fortune, saves his life, etc. The story ends with the companion's disclosing himself as the man whose corpse the other had befriended.

GRAT·I·FI·CA'·TION *noun* 1 The act of gratifying; a satisfy-ing or pleasing. 2 The state of being gratified; specifically, in psychology, the satisfaction of sexual craving. 3 That which gratifies; a reward; recompense; gratuity. See syno-nyms under HAPPINESS, SATISFACTION.

GRAT'·I·FY *tr. verb* [·FIED, ·FY·ING] 1 To please, as by sat-isfying a desire or need; indulge; humor; oblige. 2 [Obs.] To recompense, reward, or give a gratuity to. See synonyms under ENTERTAIN, INDULGE, REJOICE. [<L. *gratifico* <*gratus*, kind] — GRAT'·I·FI·ER *noun* — GRAT'·I·FY·INC

GRA·TIN (grä·täN') *noun* [F ⸱ ⸱ ⸱ned ⸱ dishes, or the method of r pared. — AU GRATIN (' as, potatoes *au grati*

GRA⸱ ⸱r. ve⸱

FUNK & WAGNALLS COMPANY

NEW YORK

From Funk & Wagnall's New Practical Standard Dictionary of the English Language, *Britannica World Language Edition, Volume One, 1955.*
The Grateful Dead—then called the Warlocks—took their name from this dictionary in 1965.

Dear Grateful Dead,

As a social worker at a community mental health agency, one of my projects includes running a music therapy program with a group of schizophrenic and severely disturbed adults. During one session, I included "Ripple" among the songs I intended to teach to the group. The results were truly surprising.

A normally passive and extremely unassertive group of people took the initiative to join in with my singing and guitar playing, and before I had the opportunity to "teach," they were singing the lyrics from the song sheets that were distributed. Afterwards, a lively and intelligent conversation ensued about some of the thoughts and feelings expressed in the song. For people who normally have great difficulty in expressing themselves, this was a really magical moment. I thought you all might enjoy hearing about another way your music has brought joy to people.

Dead Head letter
Tappan, New York, 1982

Saturday afternoon Temple Stadium, Philadelphia. Backstage is one end of the stadium marked off by a wooden snow fence. Somehow, three kids have bluffed their way back there and are talking to Jerry Garcia.

First Kid: The new album, what will it be like?

Garcia: I like it better than any album we've done.

First Kid: That's all we do is sit around and get smashed and listen to that album...

Garcia: We get smashed and make them...

Harry Jackson
Zygote, July 22, 1970

Photo by Robert Vernon Wilson © Natural Photography 1982.

one evening in the apartment, cross-legged on the floor we passed the reefers 'round. *anthem of the sun* was playing when a riff caught my attention; a glimmer of light came through. you know, I said, they could almost be the one.

but as yet I didn't see.

months later it happened. eyes closed, curled in the armchair and oblivious to living room traffic, I fell deeper and deeper into "dark star," meeting myself for the first time. and then I knew; I became a dead freak when no one else seemed to hear.

they laughed at my exclusive preference; oh it's her turn to put on the tunes—you know what *that* means.

but I was finally understanding beauty and its equivalent truth. with that vision and other awakenings I came to meditation, learning from any source that had something to give. but always the dead, they always got me high.

Dead Head letter
Boulder, Colorado, 1973

Grateful Dead: *Reckoning* **(Arista) I know you're not going to care, but I've played all of this live-acoustic twofer many times and felt no pain. Sure it's a mite leisurely, sure Jerry's voice creaks like an old floorboard, sure there are remakes if not reremakes. But the songs are great, the commitment palpable, and they always were my favorite folk group.**
B PLUS

Robert Christgau
The Village Voice, *June 24-30, 1981*

GRATEFUL DEAD

PRESENTS THREE CONCERTS

At the Sound & Light Theatre, Gizeh
on Thursday, Friday and Saturday
14, 15, and 16 September 1978
at 9:30 PM

Special Guest: HAMZA EL-DIN

Litho in U.S.A.
by San Anselmo

© 1978 Grateful Dead Productions

Gigs PRESENTA
GRATEFUL DE

LUNES 19, Octu
Palacio de los Deport

VENTA ANTICIPADA DE LOCA
EN BARCELONA: DISCO 100,
la Rambla, 15 y Tallers, 3 y 79
Balmes, 335 / TAQUILLAS
EN TARRASA: RADIO CLU
San Antonio Mª Claret, 22,

EN DISCOS
Y CASSETTES

ariola
ARISTA

To "Dead Heads" Office:
I'm very sorry we Japanese can't see the "Grateful Dead."
We are in the distance from you across the Pacific Ocean and scarcely hear of the things about you.

So please send me your peaceful information. I wait for it on the other side of the Earth.

Dead Head letter
Tokyo, Japan

To everyone in the Dead,
This is from a faraway country—India. I am a great fan of your band and your music.

You people are really mindblowing. The music you make is not really heard as it is *felt*. It flows—flows through veins in lyrical steps, very high and very calm. Like nirvana, it lends superconsciousness to the person who listens. So, I really want to thank you guys for teaching me the art of "being" with your music.

Dead Head letter
Calcutta, India, 1981

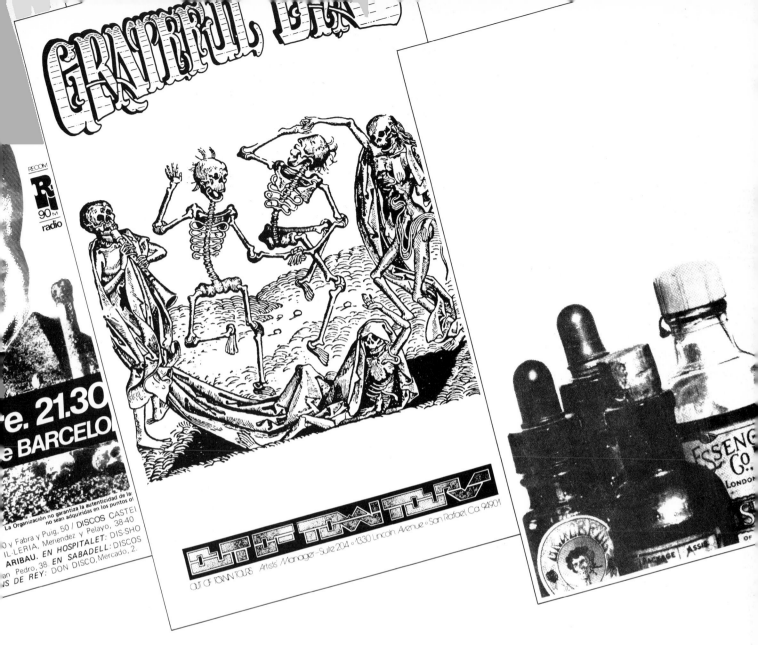

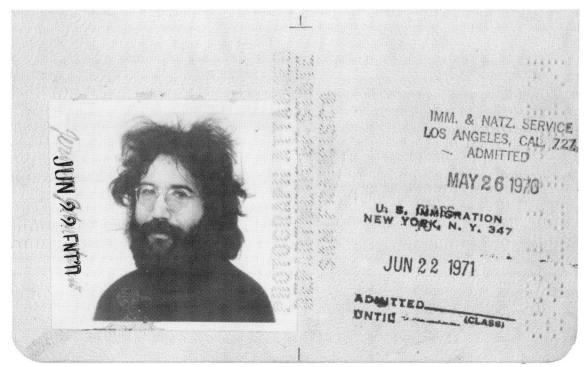

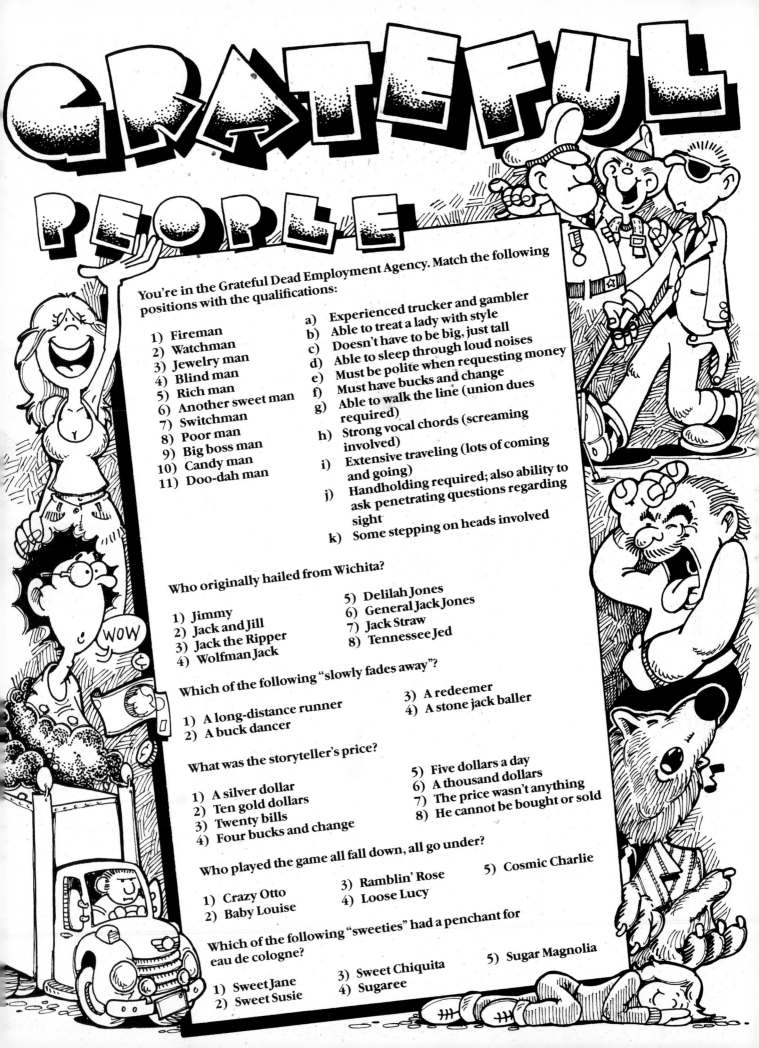

GRATEFUL PEOPLE

You're in the Grateful Dead Employment Agency. Match the following positions with the qualifications:

1) Fireman
2) Watchman
3) Jewelry man
4) Blind man
5) Rich man
6) Another sweet man
7) Switchman
8) Poor man
9) Big boss man
10) Candy man
11) Doo-dah man

a) Experienced trucker and gambler
b) Able to treat a lady with style
c) Doesn't have to be big, just tall
d) Able to sleep through loud noises
e) Must be polite when requesting money
f) Must have bucks and change
g) Able to walk the line (union dues required)
h) Strong vocal chords (screaming involved)
i) Extensive traveling (lots of coming and going)
j) Handholding required; also ability to ask penetrating questions regarding sight
k) Some stepping on heads involved

Who originally hailed from Wichita?

1) Jimmy
2) Jack and Jill
3) Jack the Ripper
4) Wolfman Jack
5) Delilah Jones
6) General Jack Jones
7) Jack Straw
8) Tennessee Jed

Which of the following "slowly fades away"?

1) A long-distance runner
2) A buck dancer
3) A redeemer
4) A stone jack baller

What was the storyteller's price?

1) A silver dollar
2) Ten gold dollars
3) Twenty bills
4) Four bucks and change
5) Five dollars a day
6) A thousand dollars
7) The price wasn't anything
8) He cannot be bought or sold

Who played the game all fall down, all go under?

1) Crazy Otto
2) Baby Louise
3) Ramblin' Rose
4) Loose Lucy
5) Cosmic Charlie

Which of the following "sweeties" had a penchant for eau de cologne?

1) Sweet Jane
2) Sweet Susie
3) Sweet Chiquita
4) Sugaree
5) Sugar Magnolia

TRIVIA

GEOGRAPHY

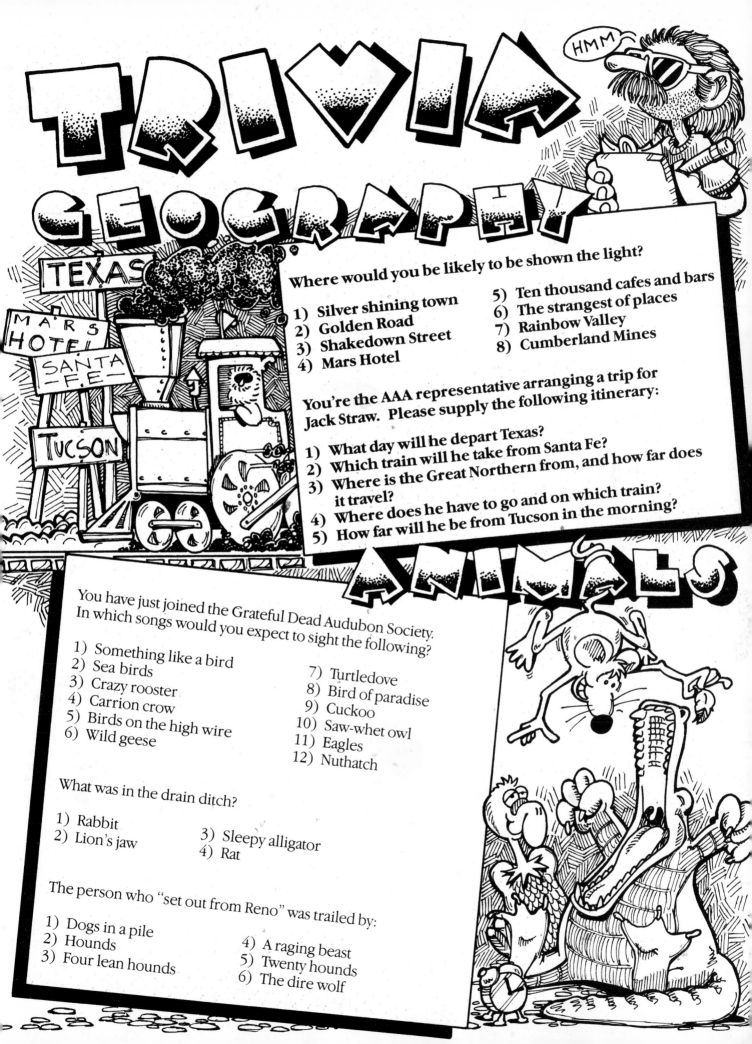

Where would you be likely to be shown the light?

1) Silver shining town
2) Golden Road
3) Shakedown Street
4) Mars Hotel
5) Ten thousand cafes and bars
6) The strangest of places
7) Rainbow Valley
8) Cumberland Mines

You're the AAA representative arranging a trip for Jack Straw. Please supply the following itinerary:

1) What day will he depart Texas?
2) Which train will he take from Santa Fe?
3) Where is the Great Northern from, and how far does it travel?
4) Where does he have to go and on which train?
5) How far will he be from Tucson in the morning?

ANIMALS

You have just joined the Grateful Dead Audubon Society. In which songs would you expect to sight the following?

1) Something like a bird
2) Sea birds
3) Crazy rooster
4) Carrion crow
5) Birds on the high wire
6) Wild geese
7) Turtledove
8) Bird of paradise
9) Cuckoo
10) Saw-whet owl
11) Eagles
12) Nuthatch

What was in the drain ditch?

1) Rabbit
2) Lion's jaw
3) Sleepy alligator
4) Rat

The person who "set out from Reno" was trailed by:

1) Dogs in a pile
2) Hounds
3) Four lean hounds
4) A raging beast
5) Twenty hounds
6) The dire wolf

GUSTATORY

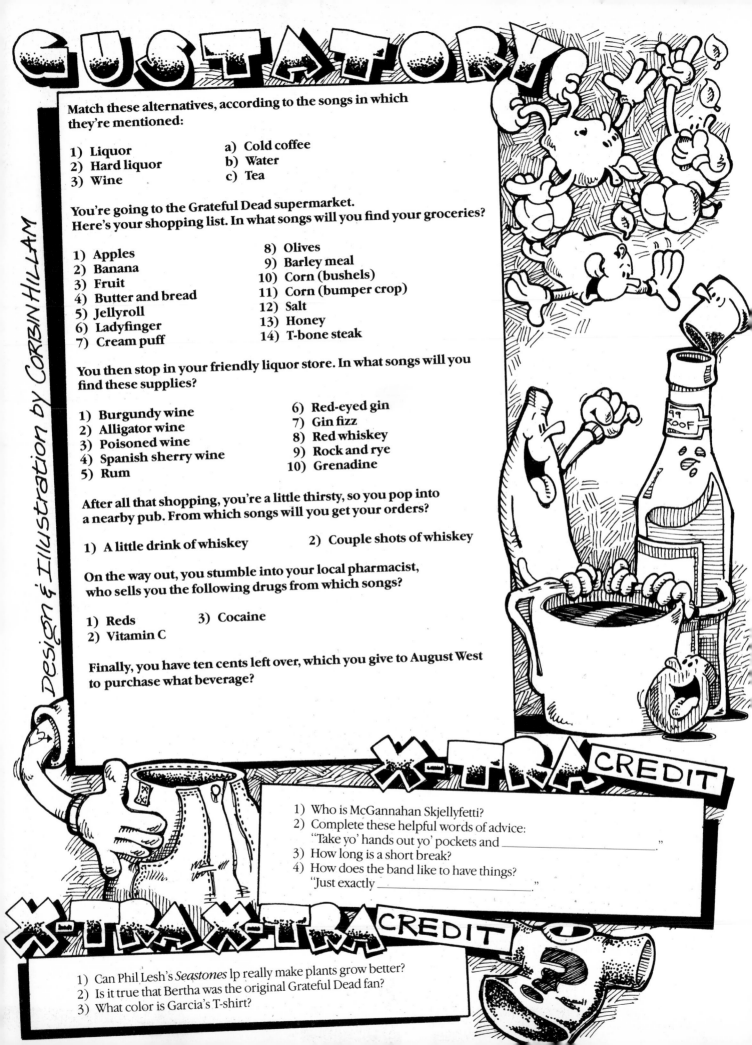

Match these alternatives, according to the songs in which they're mentioned:

1) Liquor
2) Hard liquor
3) Wine

a) Cold coffee
b) Water
c) Tea

You're going to the Grateful Dead supermarket. Here's your shopping list. In what songs will you find your groceries?

1) Apples
2) Banana
3) Fruit
4) Butter and bread
5) Jellyroll
6) Ladyfinger
7) Cream puff

8) Olives
9) Barley meal
10) Corn (bushels)
11) Corn (bumper crop)
12) Salt
13) Honey
14) T-bone steak

You then stop in your friendly liquor store. In what songs will you find these supplies?

1) Burgundy wine
2) Alligator wine
3) Poisoned wine
4) Spanish sherry wine
5) Rum

6) Red-eyed gin
7) Gin fizz
8) Red whiskey
9) Rock and rye
10) Grenadine

After all that shopping, you're a little thirsty, so you pop into a nearby pub. From which songs will you get your orders?

1) A little drink of whiskey

2) Couple shots of whiskey

On the way out, you stumble into your local pharmacist, who sells you the following drugs from which songs?

1) Reds
2) Vitamin C

3) Cocaine

Finally, you have ten cents left over, which you give to August West to purchase what beverage?

Design & Illustration by CORBIN HILLAM

X-TRA CREDIT

1) Who is McGannahan Skjellyfetti?
2) Complete these helpful words of advice:
   "Take yo' hands out yo' pockets and _____,"
3) How long is a short break?
4) How does the band like to have things?
   "Just exactly _____,"

X-TRA X-TRA CREDIT

1) Can Phil Lesh's *Seastones* lp really make plants grow better?
2) Is it true that Bertha was the original Grateful Dead fan?
3) What color is Garcia's T-shirt?

TIME LINE

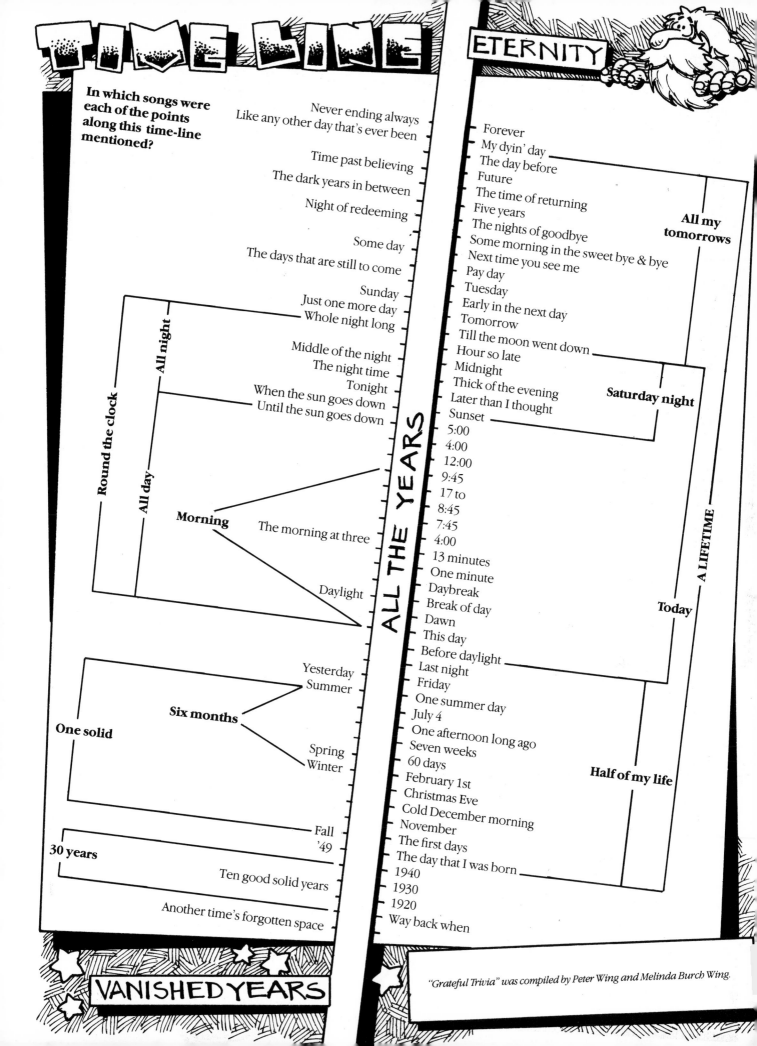

In which songs were each of the points along this time-line mentioned?

Never ending always
Like any other day that's ever been

Time past believing
The dark years in between
Night of redeeming

Some day
The days that are still to come

Sunday
Just one more day
Whole night long

Middle of the night
The night time
Tonight
When the sun goes down
Until the sun goes down

The morning at three

Daylight

Yesterday
Summer

Spring
Winter

Fall
'49

Ten good solid years

Another time's forgotten space

Round the clock
All night
All day
Morning

One solid
Six months

30 years

Forever
My dyin' day
The day before
Future
The time of returning
Five years
The nights of goodbye
Some morning in the sweet bye & bye
Next time you see me
Pay day
Tuesday
Early in the next day
Tomorrow
Till the moon went down
Hour so late
Midnight
Thick of the evening
Later than I thought
Sunset
5:00
4:00
12:00
9:45
17 to
8:45
7:45
4:00
13 minutes
One minute
Daybreak
Break of day
Dawn
This day
Before daylight
Last night
Friday
One summer day
July 4
One afternoon long ago
Seven weeks
60 days
February 1st
Christmas Eve
Cold December morning
November
The first days
The day that I was born
1940
1930
1920
Way back when

ALL THE YEARS

All my tomorrows

Saturday night

A LIFETIME

Today

Half of my life

"Grateful Trivia" was compiled by Peter Wing and Melinda Burch Wing.

It was getting time for a talk with the kid, Incredible Cosmo thought, sitting at the kitchen table. The kitchen table was a large, unfinished spool that had once been wrapped in telephone line. On the table was a large jug of extremely red wine.

Cosmo stroked his beard and thought about talking to the kid, his son. Zeke, the kid, was already 11 and growing like a bean sprout. But the kid, to Cosmo's consternation and surprise, was growing up...well, *weird*.

Zeke was into Kiss and Leif Garrett and Boston, and he had taken lately to asking Cosmo for money to have his 11-year-old hair styled.

The Incredible Cosmo ran a hand through his own frizzy corona of hair—it looked recently singed—and called the kid over. "Hey, Zeke, c'mere," Cosmo said, walking toward the cinderblock bookshelf where the stereo sat. "I got something I want you to listen to."

Zeke knew the tone in his old man's voice; it was the same coaxing wheedle he used when trying to convince his son to eat wheat germ. Zeke knew better than to eat any kind of germ.

"The new Dead album. The Grateful Dead," Cosmo said. "It's called 'Shakedown Street.' Let's listen to it."

Zeke did not know what to make of this, so he reluctantly sat on his father's bedenimed lap as the tone arm dropped into place.

"I got into the Dead just about the time you were born," Cosmo said, while Bob Weir began to chunka-chunk the rhythm part of The Rascals' *Good Lovin'*.

"The Dead were part of a whole new thing then: Kesey, Owsley, the acid tests, the Angels and Sonny, Zaps, Golden Gate Park, the Avalon and Winterland, Hunter Thompson was there, Mountain Girl with Jerry, Ripple, S. Clay Wilson, reds, the Stone when it was still good, Cassady, bikes, Krassner, Grace and Paul and Marty...."

Cosmo looked down and saw his son's face, blank as an unsold tombstone. Zeke was listening to the title track. Zeke thought it sounded like bad disco.

"The Dead, they were the first band to really, uh, to play ...like, it's, uh, intuitive music," Cosmo said. He did not like to call it acid rock; that was Life Magazine's term. "This kind of music, you have to get inside it, you know, like ah, ummmmm, you have to know what they're doing and, uh, sort of...*get there* with them, like on their plane, you know?"

Zeke clearly did not know. He was listening to *Serengetti* and he had never encountered a drum solo before, let alone a double drum solo. He looked up into his father's small, round wire-rims.

"Hey, you listen to the radio," the Incredible Cosmo said, "you got to know some Dead stuff. Like *Truckin'*. Everybody knows *Truckin'*."

Zeke did not know *Truckin'*.
I need a woman twice my height
raven-tressed, darkly blessed
a goddess of the night...
Bob Weir sang. The level of the extremely red wine had dropped in the extremely large jug. Cosmo figured the kid was beginning to get into it. Zeke was shaking one of his feet, more or less in time with Phil Lesh's burbling bass. Cosmo beamed. Zeke had to go to the bathroom.

"Hey, now check this one—*Stagger Lee*—it's the Dead's version of an old blues, not like, you know, a cover or any-

thing, but Garcia and Bob Hunter—he's the guy that writes the words, he plays bagpipes and lives in England—they wrote a new one," Cosmo said.

Stagger Lee wasn't bad, Zeke thought, boring, but not bad. Like whole wheat bread.

The tone arm had wound almost all the way across "Shakedown Street." Cosmo closed his eyes and rubbed his bald spot and hummed along to *All New Minglewood Blues.* Mickey Hart and Billy Kreutzmann were drumming together again, thumping out a primal rhythm that—with the now-vanished extremely red wine—washed the Incredible Cosmo back over the brink of the decade.

Zeke knew this death-like trance of the old man's and seized the opportunity to slip out of his lap. He lifted the tone arm off the refrain of *If I Had the World to Give* and eased the record back into the jacket.

Cosmo snored softly from dreamland, at peace with Kesey and Garcia, drinking Ripple with Pig Pen and Black Maria, comparing tattoos with Sonny and, mostly, blissing out.

Zeke, wishing his name was Randy or something like that, slipped Kiss onto the turntable and the headphones over his ears. Looking out of the corner of his eye to make sure the Incredible Cosmo was still in the sandman's hands, Zeke turned the volume up and began to try to teach himself to dance.

It's like intuitive, you know?

Guy Williams
Winston-Salem (North Carolina) Journal, *December 3, 1978*

Dear Dead Heads,

I am trying to be a poet, but since I need to eat, I'm teaching children to write poetry at one of the more open schools here in Tempe. The other day I decided to play music and tell the kids (fourth and fifth graders) to shut their eyes and let the music paint fantasies, dreams, images, and so on. What could be more appropriate, I thought, for trippy little kids than "Dark Star"? I thought you might be interested in what some of the kids wrote:

"Blue," by Nicole, age nine:
Blue is as blue as a bell ringing
Blue is as blue as the waves falling.
Blue is as blue as the smell of flowers,
Blue is as blue as drums beating.
Blue is as blue as the water in a pool.

Scott, age ten: I saw a guitar in the Orient playing itself, and skipping along with a dog playing a fiddle.

Keith, age ten: It made me feel sad and happy and mad and glad. I saw blue and green and orange and purple stars, and all different colored rockets and red lightning.

Todd, age ten: First I saw black. But then I saw little dots of white and bursts of color began to form. First red, orange, green, yellow, purple, pink, and blue. They came all at once for the last five minutes like big splashes of color that kept forming.

Dead Head letter
Tempe, Arizona, 1972

POLYNÉSIE
PARADIS PERDU

ANARCHY.

THE NEW
CONSTITUTION
OF CALIFORNIA.
KEARNEYISM,
OTHER PEOPLE
HOM
SAVIN
LAND
PROPERTY
LIVES.
CAPITAL AND
HONEST LABOR,
ALL
COMMON STOCK
IN THE UNIVERSAL
CO-OPERATIVE
BROTHERHOOD.

FREE LOVE
DEADHEADISM
COMMUNIST

NON
AIS NUCLÉAIRE
OLYNÉSIE

NO
FL

THE
DEAD
HEAD
ENTERPRISES, LTD.

ARTIFACTS FOR MIND & BODY

Mary M. Wilson, Proprietor

2759 LAKE TAHOE BOULEVARD
(next to Meek's Lumber)
P.O. Box 00 · South Lake Tahoe, CA 95729

Photo
© Frantisek Drtikol

WHOLE WHEAT

16 oz (1 lb.)

Workingman's Bread

Box 2569
Taos, New Mexico
87571

PAR AVION

Ca. 94-

A LA CENT

MANV

au NUCLEAIRE

THE HINDU DEAD-HEAD !
YOGI HATHANOGA, of Benares

Buried His Head in the Ground for 9 Hours

s one of a variety of "Samadhi," which is a
for the ecstatic religious practices of the
n. The ability to double the tongue within
completely to obstruct the nasal passage
ature of the practice.
on of the Yogi, Pratapa Hathanoga, is
photograph taken on the spot. The
statement, and the length of time the
he upside down position with his head
und, is the German traveler Paul

'Orientreisen," by Paul Deussen.
122

Grateful Bread

QUALITY BAKERY   BETHLEHEM PA

869-5847

Whole Wheat bread 1 lb. 100%
ground wheat, water, honey, yeast
safflower oil, salt

mal

To the Dead,
   We realize you have a very busy schedule, but anyway we would like to challenge you to a softball
game when you play in Atlanta next month. We are
not a professional team, just a bunch of freaks who
formed a team to flip out some rednecks, but found
out we could win if we tried. So we got really hung
up in it last summer (our first year). Our name is the
Sugar Magnolias. We played in the Athens softball
league with 87 other teams (ours was the only freak
one), ended the season with a 42 and 12 win-loss
record, and made it to the second round of the play-
offs. We came a long way in helping relationships
between us and the straights, and by midseason
we had a large following that included many local
policemen cheering for us.

Dead Head letter
Athens, Georgia, 1971

Free Estimates

Scarlet Begonias Painting
Exteriors – Interiors

Richard Reilly
Deborah Kaplan

In the Beginning, the Acid Tests

Jerry: The Acid Test was the prototype for our whole basic trip. But nothing has ever come up to the level of the way the Acid Test was. It's just never been equalled, really, or the basic hit of it never developed out. What happened was light shows and rock and roll came out of it, and that's like the thing that we've seen go out.

Reich: But what was it when it was at it's greatest?

Well, something much more incredible than just a rock and roll show with a light show; it was just a million more times incredible. It was incredible because of the formlessness, because of the thing of people wandering around wondering what was going on and...and stuff happening spontaneously and everybody bein' prepared to accept any kind of a thing that was happening and to add to it, was like... uh...

Mountain Girl: Everybody felt pretty much responsible for each other.

Reich: Everybody was doing something.

Everybody was doing everything. That's about the simplest explanation.

Reich: And it was magical besides.

Truly, it was magical because there was that willingness for everybody to be constantly on the lookout for something new.

Where was the second Acid Test?

Jerry: It was at the Big Beat, a plushy little nightclub in Palo Alto. That was a real nice one. There was the stage with the Grateful Dead setup on it over here ...The Dead's on stage and on the other side there's a kind of a long sort of a runway affair. It's sort of an L-shaped room, and on the point of the L is the Grateful Dead and down here is where the Pranksters have their setup. We'd play stuff and the Pranksters would be doin' stuff and there was this incredible cross interference and weirdness.

What happened at the end of the evening?

Jerry: This one ended up with Neil Cassady under the strobe light tearing up paper.

Mountain Girl: Tearing up his shirt! He was ripping up that beautiful fluorescent polka dot shirt that Marge Barge made him, tearing it into little pieces. And then he got onto the paper after the shirt. He was ripping up anything he could get his hands on.

Jerry: It was going very very fast and then it was very quiet; there was almost nothing else happening.

Mountain Girl: Right, except all the equipment was on and it was humming and any noise was sort of weirdly echoed around.

Jerry: And amplified around..

Mountain Girl: And so it was sort of strange in there. A lot of people were drifting in and out of the spotlight and the strobe light was stopped and sort of the falling dance was going on, you know, people were still on their feet and meandering around.

Jerry: And it's getting to be about dawn.

Mountain Girl: Yeah, people start to step outside to check the air, you know...

Jerry: Real cold in the morning...

Mountain Girl: After an Acid Test was always morning. You start to pack up and step outside and it would be cold there and, ohhhh, really clear and everybody looking about eight inches shorter than they had been...

Charles Reich and Jann Wenner
Rolling Stone, *January 20, 1972*

Mountain Girl and Jerry Garcia, circa 1967. Photo by Herb Greene.

Tom Snyder, Ken Kesey and Jerry Garcia on Tomorrow, *1981. Photo by Chuck Pulin.*

Third Acid Test, Muir Beach

The third Acid Test was scheduled for Stinson Beach, 15 miles north of San Francisco. Stinson Beach was already a gathering place for local heads. You could live all winter in little beach cottages there for next to nothing. There was a nice solid brick recreation hall on the beach, all very nice—but at the last minute that whole deal fell through, and they shifted to Muir Beach, a few miles south. The handbills were already out, all over the head sections of San Francisco, CAN *YOU* PASS THE ACID TEST, advertising Cassady & Ann Murphy Vaudeville and celebrities who *might be* there, which included anybody who happened to be in town, or might make it to town, the Fugs, Ginsberg, Roland Kirk. There were always some nice chiffon subjunctives and the future conditionals in the Prankster handbill rhetoric, but who was to deny who *might be* drawn into the Movie…

Anyway, at the last minute they headed for Muir Beach instead. The fact that many people wouldn't know about the change and would go to Stinson Beach and merely freeze in the darkness and never find the right place—somehow that didn't even seem distressing. It was part of some strange analogical order of the universe. Norman Hartweg hooked down his LSD—it was in the acid gas capsules that night—and thought of Gurdjieff. Gurdjieff wouldn't announce a meeting until the last minute. We're gonna get together tonight. The people that got there, got there; and there was message in that alone. Which was, of course: *you're either on the bus or off the bus.*

Those who were on the bus, even if they weren't Pranksters, like Marshall Efron, the round Mercury of Hip California, or the Hell's Angels…all found it. The cops, however, never did. They were apparently thrown off by the Stinson Beach handbills.

Muir Beach had a big log-cabin-style lodge for dances, banquets, and the like. The lodge was stilted up out in a waste of frigid marsh grass. A big empty nighttime beach in winter. Some little log tourist cabins with blue doors on either side, all empty. The lodge had three big rooms and was about 100 feet long, all logs and rafters and exposed beams, a tight ship of dark wood and Roughing It. The Grateful Dead piled in with their equipment and the Pranksters with theirs, which now included a Hammond electric organ for Gretch and a great strobe light.

Practically everybody who has found the place, after the switch from Stinson Beach, is far enough into the thing to know what the "acid" in the Acid Test means. A high percentage took LSD about four hours ago, rode out the first rush and are ready…now to groove….The two projectors shine forth with The Movie. The bus and the Pranksters start rolling over the walls of the lodge, Babbs and Kesey rapping on about it, the Bus lumping huge and vibrating and bouncing in great swells of heads and color—Norman, zonked, sitting on the floor, is half frightened, half ecstatic, although something in the back of his mind recognizes this as his Acid Test pattern, to sit back and watch, holding on through the rush, until 3 or 4 A.M., in the magic hours, and then dance—but so much of a rush this time! The Movie and Roy Seburn's light machine pitching the intergalactic red science-fiction seas to all corners of the lodge, oil and water and food coloring pressed between plates of glass and projected in vast size so that the very ooze of cellular Creation seems to ecto-plast into the ethers and then the Dead coming in with their immense submarine vibrato vibrating, *garanging,* from the Aleutian rocks to the baja griffin cliffs of the Gulf of California. The Dead's weird sound! agony-in-ecstasis! submarine somehow, turbid half the time, tremendously loud but like sitting under a waterfall, at the same time full of sort of ghoul-show vibrato sounds as if each string on their electric guitars is half a block long and twanging in a room full of natural gas, not to mention their great Hammond electric organ, which sounds like a movie house Wurlitzer, a diathermy machine, a Citizens' Band radio and an Auto-Grind garbage truck at 4 A.M., all coming over the same frequency…

Tom Wolfe
The Electric Kool-Aid Acid Test, *1968*

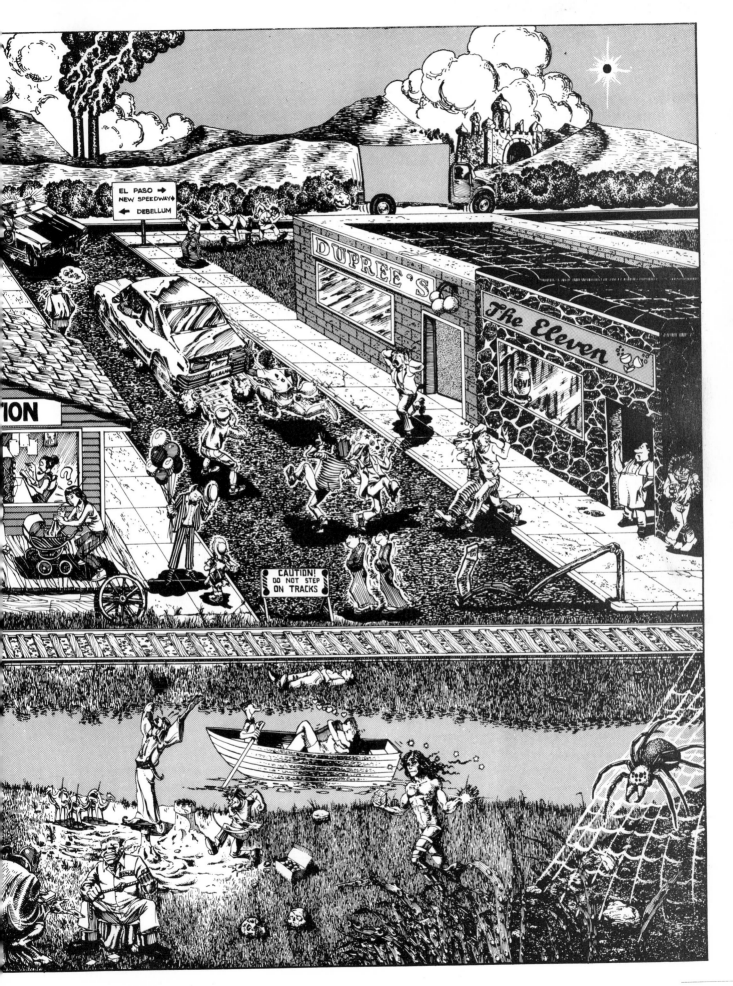

The common ground between the Dead and the young Dead Heads is the belief that the way to meet an impossible circumstance is with voluntary craziness.

Charlie Haas
New West, *December 17, 1979*

DEAD POEM

In concert halls, Nirvana?
Sleeping Beauty and Sleeping Ghost Dance 'round Messiah Purples/
Art in the Blood/
Dancing feet in time with Star Wars and Emotion jerking the
Soul with Panic Questions: "Is it truly Me?"
Lifesand slipping into Tomorrow-Wants/Now.
The sprite Joy-Dance of individual energies harmonizing
in the Breath of Earth-Being.

SpaceMan says:
It's circus-time for the mind/
Blue drifters in New Horizon/
Rhythm Devils of Beat in the Tundra of Madness/
Winds shiver the spine in the twilight of Discovery:
Dead Concerts are Heaven on Earth!
(for a brief moment)

Charging out at the Night/
Finding lovers in the maze of the Revolution/
Evolution of the American Spirit/
Hanging on the The Dream/
Pristine petals of Caesar/
We are All-One.

This isn't rock 'n roll, this is blown out
Cinema at the Freedom Flow America.
Choose our heroes in these metal days.
Peace and Resolution in the power of Harmony and Discord/
Beauty in the Dark Corner of Fear/
Relief in the desirable journey of Unknown/
Happiness in finding home.

Peter Asmus
Winds of Change, *April, 1982*

Jerry Garcia *in concert* **Mickey Hart**

Palace of Fine Arts Auditorium · Wednesday November 28, 7pm. Also The Mantric Sun Band and The Sat Nam Singers.

Reich: Who's the audience now? Who are the magic people?

Jerry: The magic people are out living productive lives, working on things, doing things—post-revolutionary activities, and women are out raising the kids. I think we have a whole range now for an audience and the reason we have the range is because of the popularity of our most recent records. We have grandmothers! and grandfathers! All kinds of people that come and get off and are happy to have been there.

Reich: But they all believe in magic, wouldn't you say?

Jerry: That's a generalization I hate to make. It's too spotty. Some scenes we've played at that have been expressly for people to get high in—for example, the spiritual trips that haven't been advertised as rock and roll concerts—bring the kind of people who know what it is to get high and are thus able to participate in that way and really get high. The times we've played at spiritual things have been our most hits, when people are there to get high. I think basically the Grateful Dead is not for cranking out rock and roll, it's not for going out and doing concerts or any of that stuff, I think it's to get high.

Reich: Why is it important to get high? Why is it important to stay high?

What good does it do anybody—the world, the community or people themselves?

Jerry: To get really high is to forget yourself. And to forget yourself is to see everything else. And to see everything else is to become an understanding molecule in evolution, a conscious tool of the universe. And I think every human being should be a conscious tool of the universe. That's why I think it's important to get high.

Reich: Getting zonked out or unconscious is a whole different thing.

Jerry: I'm not talking about unconscious or zonked out, I'm talking about being fully conscious. Also I'm not talking about the Grateful Dead as being an end in itself. I don't think of that highness as being an end in itself. I think of the Grateful Dead as being a crossroads or a pointer sign and what we're pointing to is that there's a lot of universe available, that there's a whole lot of experience available over here. We're kinda like a signpost, and we're *also* pointing to danger, to difficulty, we're pointing to bummers. We're pointing to whatever there is, when we're on—when it's really happening.

You're a signpost to new space?

Jerry: Yes. That's the place where we should be—that's the function we should be filling in society. And in our own little society, that's the function we

do fill. But in the popular world—the media world and so forth—we're just a rock and roll band.

We play rock and roll music and it's part of our form—our vehicle so to speak—but it's not who we are totally. Like Moondog in New York City who walks around, he's a signpost to otherness. He's a signpost to something that isn't concrete. It's that same thing.

Where did you get the idea about pointing to some new place.

Jerry: We never formulated it, it just was what was happening. We were doing the Acid Test, which was our first exposure to formlessness. Formlessness and chaos lead to new forms. And new order. Closer to, probably, what the real order is. When you break down the old orders and the old forms and leave them broken and shattered, you suddenly find yourself a new space with new form and new order which are more like the way it is. More like the flow.

Charles Reich and Jann Wenner
Rolling Stone, *February 3, 1972*

Question Man

How Do You Meet Nice Guys in This Town?

Wendy Halverson, bill collector, Market street:
Go to a rock concert and get good and lost. That's what I did. I met a really nice guy at this one rock concert and we're still together. I am from West Virginia and when I first came out here I didn't know anybody. I went to a Grateful Dead concert and I walked up to him and asked for a bite of his celery stalk.

San Francisco Chronicle
Date unknown

Student Appalled

To the Editor:

Graduation is the day of the student. It is both the end and the beginning. Graduation is something a student dreams about. Graduation day is a day that parents should be proud of their children no matter how they act. It shouldn't matter to a parent if the song playing during the graduation march is by the Grateful Dead. The only thing that should matter is that your son or daughter is going to receive his or her diploma, and I feel you should be pretty happy about just that in itself, and not worry yourselves about anything else.

To all my fellow students, I am proud to have graduated with you. We did it the right way.

Brandon DeHaven
Cranford (NJ)

Letter to the editor
Cranford (New Jersey) Citizen and Chronicle, *July 3, 1979*

Letters

Dear folks,

Just a note. I had recently been lining the bottom of my parakeets' cage with the editorial page from the State Journal. They became hostile and constantly screeched at each other. I tried using your last issue with Jerry Garcia. Good Lord! They coo like lovebirds now.

We thank you,
Red and friends.

Ditto... we think.

To the Dead:

Just in case you have a file for miscellaneous, useless information, you might be interested in knowing that there's a professional stunt pilot (me) with a stereo tape system geared to play through the earphones in his crash helmet (with a radio cut-out switch). While I'm going through loops, rolls, spins, and so on, in front of cameras or crowds of thousands, I'm quite contentedly hanging by my seat belts listening to "Truckin'" or some such.

If I can ever figure a way to sync the tape deck in my plane with the same tape playing through an airshow P.A. system, I want to work out an aerial ballet to music, preferably Dead or, perhaps, a Bach fugue.

Dead Head letter
Colorado Springs, Colorado, 1974

At the top of Donohue Pass, 11,056 feet above sea level, a dude comes floating along with a beard and long hair and purple Coke-bottle shades. He floats right by with a nod, sees Bill Walton's Grateful Dead shirt and mutters, "Hey, how's the band?"

A Deadhead!

Walton nearly falls off his rock. "Grrrreat!" he says, just like Tony the Tiger. A while later, Walton catches up to the guy—his name is Dave—and stops to chat. "I think I've seen you before," Dave says to Walton.

"Probably at a Grateful Dead concert," says Walton.

"Yeah, I guess so," says Dave.

Fruit is shared, and the two talk the language of the Dead.

"I know I've seen you," says Dave.

"At a Grateful Dead concert, I'm telling you," says Walton, playing Dave to the hilt.

Dave snaps his fingers. "Were you at the concert in Pauley the day before New Year's?"

"Yep."

"Were you one of the guys dancing around on stage when that Egyptian guy was singing?"

"Yep."

"That's where I saw you!" says Dave, satisfied.

John Papanek
Sports Illustrated, *October 15, 1979*

Grateful Dead concerts are like baseball games: no two are ever alike. The plays are always different, and there's always fresh hope. Sometimes the game's an all-timer even though individual performances are sloppy; sometimes everybody plays great but the team loses anyway.

Some people thrive on yesterday's moments, and aren't too keen on the way the game's played today. Some have only been fans since last year and don't care what happened way back when. You can cherish the great victories and triumphant seasons and chart them across decades, or you can go simply for the enjoyment of tonight and to hell with the standings. Like all the great teams, the Dead have their pennant years and bleak innings, perfect games and whippings, hits and foul balls, heroes and goats.

To many they're an institution, to some mere child's play, and to others the Grateful Dead is more or less an indispensable part of life. There are those who say the game's too slow, that the brief moments of action and excitement are too few and far between. Like America's Favorite Pastime, the Dead are both celebrated and criticized, and as with the Great National Sport, some people will never see what's to enjoy.

Like big-league fans, Dead Heads are as varied as the game is long. There are score-keepers who record every detail for statistical analysis and a place in the Hall of Fame; camera buffs and video freaks; armchair umpires, die-hards, *groupies.* Some are

Photo by Robert Ve....

bleacher bums who'd be in the stands no matter who was playing; and there are even spousal fans who go because if they didn't, they'd be left home alone. A lot of people attend because they've always gone and really don't care to stop.

It may take a few visits to grasp the subtleties, but if you let yourself into the flow of things, there's something to enjoy from the very first moment you're there. As the old saying goes, the mind believes what the mind believes: Grateful Dead is cerebral if you choose to analyze it, but it's basic and instinctive too. Like the game of baseball.

*David Gans
1981*

To the Dead:

This concerns the song "The Music Never Stopped" and Cow Dancing.

Last spring, my boyfriend took me up to Sonoma Mountain and showed me the Cow Dance. No one else knows the steps or can attempt at duplicating this sacred dance. He said he can only do this in the presence of cows. It is a ceremonial dance in praise of our bovine sisters and brothers who rule the celestial fields of the Sonoma Mountains.

The next time, upon listening to "The Music Never Stopped," I realized that the beginning of the song had captured the very essence of Cow Dancing. Wow. Maybe you *do* know something about Cow Dancing!

Anyway…August 22nd is Cow Day.

Dead Head letter
Cotati, California, 1979

To the Dead,

We had a dog named Underdog. He was a scrapper, but he had to be. Abandoned, shifting for himself when he was a puppy, his life was hard. Then we found him and his life was a little easier, but not much. We moved a lot, and his security was broken many times. But his spirit grew, and he became a member of our group of friends. He was truly an *Underdog,* and *he never gave up.* His tail was as high as a pup's.

Underdog died July 5. The following Tuesday, our group of friends saw you play in Kansas City. During the first set, my husband yelled out, "Play one for *Under!*" Your next song was Jerry singing "To Lay Me Down." It really hit home for all of us, and we considered it a tribute for a friend who was gone. The spirit really came through, and we thought you'd like to know about it.

Dead Head letter
1981

Dear Lou,

My LOVELIGHT shines brightly for you tonight, bright as a star, a DARK STAR in the heavens. I miss you very much, and TILL THE MORNING COMES, I'll lie here in bed knowing that while we're apart our love will NOT FADE AWAY.

Did you decide what to do with the Volkswagen? Is HELP ON THE WAY, finally? I KNOW YOU, RIDER Lou, and it's time to get THE OTHER ONE (the Rabbit) you wanted—as soon as we can raise the MONEY (MONEY!). Our old bug really is a FRIEND OF THE DEVIL! Face it, we got a bad DEAL; with all the repairs lately, it's proving to be a real LOSER. And it was always too HARD TO HANDLE, anyway.

Remember, Lou, even with a good OPERATOR at THE WHEEL, DEATH DON'T HAVE NO MERCY when you're GOIN' DOWN THE ROAD. Please, darling, drive with CAUTION. And yes, IT HURTS ME TOO, thinking about selling it, but it's NOBODY'S FAULT BUT MINE,

since I originally picked it out. Like you, I USED TO LOVE HER.

This sure is getting to be a long business trip! I miss sitting under the SUGAR MAGNOLIA in our backyard, and smelling the SCARLET BEGONIAS and the RAMBLIN' ROSE bush growing near THE ELEVEN tall pines. I wish I were getting out of bed early tomorrow to taste the SUGAREE and refreshing MORNING DEW, and oh, just to

have the sweet SATISFACTION of hearing the BIRD SONG, carrying throughout the house on the slightest RIPPLE of an EASY WIND.

By the way, did it take you long to coax that black CHINA CAT (SUNFLOWER, as we know him affectionately) down from neighbor Jim FRANKLIN'S TOWERing elm? Jim is definitely a weird guy, and so's his gardener, MR. CHARLIE. Remember that mean DIRE WOLF

they kept, called BLACK PETER? I recall when ROSEMARY, our LITTLE RED ROOSTER, tangled with him, and even MAMA TRIED to break it up—along with your sister BERTHA, who was bitten on

Good For
THOUSANDS
Of Impressions

the leg. HEAVEN HELP THE FOOL who got too close to *that* beast!

I just got back from an excursion to EL PASO, where I saw UNCLE JOHN'S BAND play in that BROKEDOWN PALACE they call the Civic. It was great—THE MUSIC NEVER STOPPED, truly an UNBROKEN CHAIN of classic tunes. Good FEEDBACK in the second set, and afterwards I saw hundreds of people DANCIN' IN THE STREET. You know who's PLAYING IN THE BAND now? Some new guy on harmonica called COSMIC CHARLIE; a rhythm guitarist named JOHNNY B. GOODE from TENNESSEE; JED Thaxton (JACK STRAW's old buddy) on drums, and his sweet

BROWN-EYED WOMAN, Margaret, singing harmony. During the break, I went backstage and asked her, "WHAT'S BECOME OF THE BABY, PRETTY PEGGY?" "O—HE'S GONE to stay with my brother Ben," she replied, "a BIG BOSS MAN in FRANCE."

Y'know, I FEEL LIKE A STRANGER in this town. Come tomorrow, I'll be ON THE ROAD

AGAIN. I leave for ALABAMA—GETAWAY first thing in the morning. My bus leaves from TERRAPIN STATION, a bit of a walk from my hotel here at the corner of THE GOLDEN ROAD and SHAKEDOWN STREET. At least this trip I'm riding as a PASSENGER, and not TRUCKIN' through the back roads of Louisiana with you, driving AROUND AND AROUND for so long I was beginning to feel BORN CROSS-EYED! But remember in Baton Rouge how we saw that dead ALLIGATOR down by CASEY JONES' WHARF? (RATs! My typewriter ribbon's giving out.)

Well, it's ONE MORE SATURDAY NIGHT, and I suppose I ought to BEAT IT ON DOWN THE LINE, as the saying goes. HIGH TIME I drew this letter to a close, else my CRAZY FINGERS won't hit the right keys. COMES A TIME when I just want TO LAY ME DOWN, y'know? There's a TV movie I think I'll fall asleep to—THE GREATEST STORY EVER TOLD, starring Hopalong CASSIDY.

I must say it smells *wonderful* in my room—IT MUST HAVE BEEN THE ROSES you sent, or maybe it's the feeling from the storm approaching—WEATHER REPORT says it LOOKS LIKE RAIN, possibly some COLD RAIN AND SNOW.

By the way, NEXT TIME YOU SEE ME, we MIGHT AS WELL take a few days off to ROW JIMMY across the BIG RIVER to MINGLEWOOD for a nice WALK IN THE SUN-SHINE. I'm really sorry I missed his birthday, but I found him a NEW POTATO CABOOSE for his train set, at the same store I bought a beautiful CHINA DOLL for ALTHEA.

I NEED A MIRACLE to get through tomorrow. All this travel-ing—THE SAME THING, over and over. Lou, sometimes I just have to say, AIN'T IT CRAZY?!

Much GOOD LOVIN',
Barbara Lewit

Letter to the editor, revised
Dead Relix, *January-February, 1976*

Second Set

Pigpen at the Fillmore East, New York. Photo by Chuck Pulin.

Some time during the break in Friday night's Grateful Dead concert, I found my way outside, to the ramp that curls up the side of Hampton Coliseum. I could see a radio tower, covered with red warning lights, rising like a needle into a velvet sky blinking with stars. To the right, in the parking lot, carnival rides went round and round, the searing neon of the Ferris wheel beckoning, fusing with the echoes of barkers on the midway.

I turned to Lucy Brown, best pal and mother of my children, who was annoyed with my need for a respite from the scene inside.

"Well, what do you think?" I asked her.

Her opinion was important, especially at this moment when I was trying to decide whether to leave and protect my sanity, or go back into that mass of milling, shuffling Dead-heads, trapped on a way station between sets. Most were doped beyond human recognition, waiting for the band to come back and return them all to some Rock and Roll cosmos.

"I'm going back in there," Lucy said. "It's all how you look at it."

We went inside, back to The Planet of the Apes. The coliseum in that garish light seemed like an intergalactic Mothership loaded with 14,000 lunatics headed for the edge of the universe.

The music started again.

We sat down, somewhere high and in the back near the "W" section, and I decided to go ahead and enjoy it.

Identification breakdown had already begun, in the first set, and this Southern crowd had given itself to the band,

letting its mind go, allowing the Dead to do whatever it wanted. Garcia's guitar playing was surreal, masterful. Phil Lesh and Bob Weir were so closely tied to him that the fast licks and slowdowns seemed choreographed. Keyboardist Brent Mydland's playing, especially in the long, improvised sways and delicate transitions, was *breathtaking*. The famed musical conversation which characterizes a Dead concert was on.

In the second set, the band began the sequence of dreamy, timeless musical journeys, including a 15-minute drum solo by Kreutzmann and Hart that was nothing short of spectacular. The two had a wall of drums, from snares to kettles, and they beat them standing up, moving back and forth along the wall, caught in strange light changes, which made them appear as tiny figures trapped in a series of small rooms.

"Feel like a Stranger" came next, and then "Wharf Rat." They finished with "U.S. Blues," and the lights came on and it was over. The crowd was nearly silent, dazed, as it walked out into the night breeze, greeted by the jolly vision of the carnival.

A young kid, no more than 17, was shouting at his friend. "Who were those guys, jeeze? I never *heard* of them before this week, jeeze!"

A man nearby, who overheard, told him: "They aren't like that all the time. That's why people follow them all up and down their tours. Just for one night like this."

But, then, it's all how you look at it.

John Coit
The Virginian-Pilot, *May 4, 1981*

◄ *Preceding page: Photo by Jerry Coughlan,* The Vancouver (Washington) Columbian.

Photo by Jim Marshall.

Photo by Jerilyn Brandelius.

Photo by Bob Marks.

Photo by Bob Marks.

Photo by Ken Friedman.

Photo by Mary Ann Mayer.

Photo by John Werner.

Above left: Breaking in San Francisco's Moscone Center, the Dead play a benefit for Vietnam Vets, May 28, 1982.

Above right: Phil Lesh, Mickey Hart, Bill Kreutzmann joined by master percussionist Airto.

Below left: The Grateful Dead at Tivoli Gardens, Copenhagen, Denmark, April, 1972.

Below right: Producer Bill Graham coming in for a landing at the traditional Winterland New Year's bash, San Francisco, 1977.

Photo by Richard McCaffrey.

The closing of Fillmore West, San Francisco, July, 1971. Photo by Jim Marshall.

The Dead came back on at Winterland, their tribal community flowing with them until, like some huge horde of lemmings, they covered the stage. There are more people on stage when the Dead play than ever got there to embrace Mick Jagger. Bill Graham, who had been dancing while Mongo Santamaria played, was back on stage grooving to the Dead. Marty Balin and Grace Slick came out from behind the curtains and sat down in back of the band in the empty row of chairs.

Sunshine and several other little tow-headed kids were on stage and the Dead's chicks were dancing like hippie go-go girls. They did a long set, "Anthem of the Sun" and "Alligator" and "Death Don't Have No Mercy" and the drum solos and cherry bomb explosions made it wild. A guy walked along the aisle selling fluorescent yo-yo's for a dollar. Sinking into the chair behind me a long-haired buckskin type sighed out "Ahhhhhhhm so stoned!!" and a man in long white robes walked slowly through the strobe light raising his hands as it flickered over him. Some of the dancers stood in one place moving up and down and raising their arms. Rock Scully, the Dead's manager, went zooming off into the crowd dancing. You could see his eyes shining 20 feet away.

The Dead did their encore and it was already two o'clock. So Bill Graham went to the microphone and said, "It's two A.M. and the law says we must close. You are all now at a private party." And he locked the doors.

So the Airplane came on after the Dead's set and their encore. And they did it. They really did it. I mean they *played*!

When it was all over, a young man said to me, with tears—literally—in his eyes, "Why can't it be like this everywhere?" I looked at him and said I wished I knew the answer.

Why not? Why not? Why not indeed?

Ralph J. Gleason
Rolling Stone, *July 12, 1969*

◄ *Photo by Bob Marks.*

11:59

*The audience was having their heads
fucked over,* knew *they were having
their heads fucked over, and loving
every minute of it.*

Alice Polesky
Changes, June 15, 1970

12:00

12:01
Happy New Year!

The closing of Winterland, San Francisco, December 31, 1978.

KENNY WARDELL: Why don't you give us a good Grateful Dead story.

BILL GRAHAM: I don't think they would object because it happened many, many years ago in the lightning days, the acid days, the mid-60's when some people did a lot of experimenting with their bodies and their souls. And some, I guess, continue to do that.

Anyway, in the early days, whenever they played the Fillmore, I was always concerned that if there's anybody on the premises that was going to be straight to relate to the world of reality, it had to be me. What I did in my private life was my private life. On the job, it was my responsibility to make sure that somebody knew the difference between the street and the curb on the sidewalk. I wanted to be "clean," so to speak, clearheaded.

Of course, it became sort of a joke with some of the groups, "Come on Bill, have a drink," and especially with The Grateful Dead. It even got to the point at one time in those days, that when The Grateful Dead played the Fillmore, my wife gave me a thermos and made me a boxed lunch, and we put a waxed stamp on it. I also used to drink a lot of 7-Up in those days, but it was closed or canned. Many gigs went by and they'd say, "Come on Bill, come on," and I'd say "Thank you gentlemen, but pass."

Then one night I went into the dressing room, like I always did, and I picked up a can of 7-Up. And what someone had done was put a hypodermic needle through all of the canned drinks and put a little bit of "goodies" inside! I opened one of the 7-Up's and

I drank it…maybe a half hour before they got on stage, I was the Lone Ranger and Tonto in one. Mickey Hart asked me if I wanted to join them on the stage for some merriment and he gave me a drumstick. For the next three and a half hours, I conducted The Grateful Dead orchestra, and probably lovingly made an ass of myself. I was on stage with musicians I respect, and who I really cared about, and care about now. And, I can tell my children I conducted The Grateful Dead.

Kenny Wardell
KMEL/Bill Graham Presents: Northern California Concert, Sports & Entertainment Guide, *1981*

Peter Barsotti (left) and Rock Scully.
Photo by Richard McCaffrey. ➤

One kid stands near the stage, staring at the equipment. His thick black hair is a tangle of knots. He's wiping his bare chest with his wrinkled shirt.

"I can't believe it," he mutters. "I can't believe it. Unbelievable. I can't believe it."

A friend comes to him, placing an arm on his shoulder and offering him some water from a canteen.

"Believe it," he says. "That's the Dead."

Jay Saporita
The Aquarian Weekly, *June 30-July 14, 1976*

Where are your children, parents? They're out on an evening with the Grateful Dead, blitzed on acid and changing overnight, while you worry about them being raped or something.

Patrick Carr
The Village Voice, *April 6, 1972*

I want to tell you about a girl I saw Saturday night. She was over on the other side of the Spectrum, a hundred yards away or more. Except for the green and red spotlights aimed at the stage, the hall was dark and she was silhouetted in one of the wide gateways that open out on the second tier. She danced alone: as if in a vision she swayed, with a motion like a graceful, trembling leaf. She was wearing a long, full skirt and it swung loosely with her body; her braided hair and long strings of beads were blurred flashes of motion caught in the light; her arms rotated like a windmill and her legs went up and down in exaggerated strides.

She looked as she might have looked in 1967, if she had been in San Francisco and danced in Golden Gate Park, and it was a strange and magical thing to see.

Out in the corridors dozens of people dressed in tie-dyed clothing were gently swaying, with bright paint on their faces and soft shoes and long hair and beads and berets, like tall grass bent by an insistent wind blowing out of the past. They were very young people. Not the people who would have remembered when all this happened first, who would have to be in their 30s now if they did.

Whether you were there and look back through a certain nostalgic haze, or whether you perceive it through the mythologies which have arisen in the intervening years, the mid-sixties must cast a special spell. The Dead—being of that time and place, or present at the creation, so to speak—perhaps have the benefit of that.

Bruce Nixon
The Trenton (New Jersey) Times, *May 4, 1981*

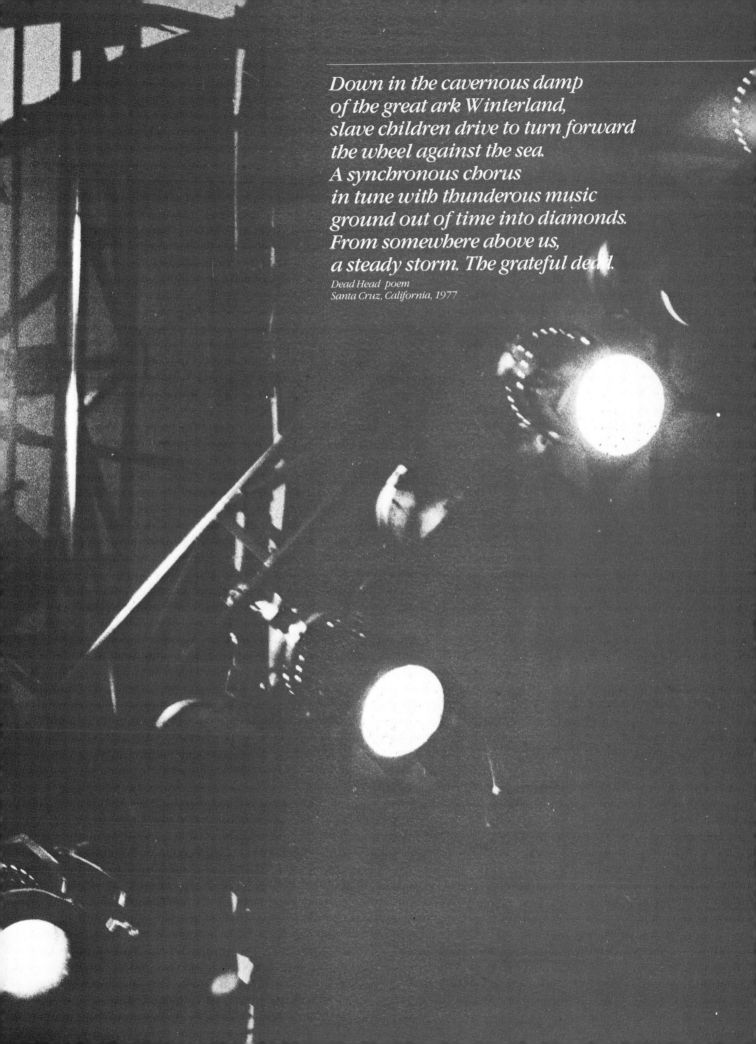

*Down in the cavernous damp
of the great ark Winterland,
slave children drive to turn forward
the wheel against the sea.
A synchronous chorus
in tune with thunderous music
ground out of time into diamonds.
From somewhere above us,
a steady storm. The grateful dead.*

*Dead Head poem
Santa Cruz, California, 1977*

Photo by Richard McCaffrey.

**Second Set Notes
by Paul Grushkin**

The "short break"
didn't seem too long this time
what with time flying
when you're with friends
happy and contented
but we are definitely ready
for much more music

suddenly the houselights fade
people anxiously step forward
heads erect, ears straining
everyone attending
the second set

ON THE DAY WHEN I WAS BORN
DADDY SAT DOWN AND CRIED

"MISSISSIPPI HALF-STEP"

a *splendid* beginning
timely and timeless
tonight's anthematic journey
intimacy born of familiarity
a symphony of undulation
we gleefully assent
breathing, bowing in unison
a form of natural timekeeping
buoyed by Lesh's constant attention
"the erudite, strong backbone"

Dear Bob Weir (through Dead Heads),
    We are deeply concerned about your lovely ass. We've always admired it. We loved your ponytail, too, but it was alright when you cut it off. Maybe you should lose a little of your ass, too. You can easily overdo that kind of good thing! We've noticed at the last couple of concerts we've been to that you've been adding ass. Is it beer? Wine? Munchies? Whatever…keep in mind that what makes an ass attractive is the lack of it.
    A word to the sexy should be sufficient.

Dead Head letter
1973

(another inimitable Graham quote)
yes, lots of memories tonight!

FAREWELL TO YOU
OLD SOUTHERN SKIES
I'M ON MY WAY

psychedelic wonderland
greets pure folk melody
we are hearing *everything*

ACROSS THE RIO GRANDE-O
ACROSS THAT LAZY RIVER

stricken with wonder
glistening in joyful beads of sweat
I'm thinking to myself
***this* is why I come to Dead concerts**
such a unity of purpose here
everyone's heart going out
in multitronic a cappella

***into* "FRANKLIN'S TOWER"**

oh, so dear to my heart
rrrrrrrringing with an urgency
crisp, insistent, almost brutal
dead on target

MAY THE FOUR WINDS
BLOW YOU SAFELY HOME

You've called them a magic band. What's the criterion?

David Crosby: Magic is doin' it so well that you get it up beyond mechanical levels. Magic is making people feel good and stuff. Magic is, if you're high on psychedelics, having a great big love beast crawl out of your amplifiers and eat the audience. I don't know what it is, man. Like, they're magic. Something happens when the Dead gets it on that don't happen when Percy Faith gets it on.

Ben Fong-Torres
Rolling Stone, July 23, 1970

Photo by Bob Marks.

Garcia lashes out
decisive short strokes
going for the viscera
friends Peter and Melinda
jigging in a circle, grinning
hugging on the fly

WHICHEVER WAY YOUR
PLEASURE TENDS
IF YOU PLANT ICE
YOU'RE GONNA HARVEST WIND!

yyyyyeeeeeoooooowwwww!!
look at everyone jump for joy
what a party
every god-blessed piece in place
and deliriously crazed
Bill Walton would be proud
—this is his all-time favorite

into "ESTIMATED PROPHET"

people edge into it

seduced by the new beat

MY TIME COMIN' ANY DAY
DON'T WORRY 'BOUT ME NOW

it suckers you in, and then *blam*

CALIFORNIA!
PREACHIN' ON THE
BURNING SHORE

all this roaring and shouting
Bobby bucking, rearing, spitting
a man with a *mission*

FIRE WHEEL
BURNING IN THE AIR

gospel for madmen
brazen and unmerciful

MIGHT AND GLORY
GONNA BE MY NAME
AND MEN GONNA LIGHT MY WAY

but just as suddenly
the torch is snuffed
and the music is again
lulling, soothing, liquid
save for Weir's barks and cries
ha *ha*
how are we to keep perspective?

"HE'S GONE"

cooling winds of sanity
back to the believable, I guess

RAT IN A DRAIN DITCH
CAUGHT ON A LIMB

but does anything make sense?
the Dead's lyrics offer no clue
—or rather
as many clues as you'd like
enigmatic rays of hope
music for bemusement

158 *Grateful Dead*

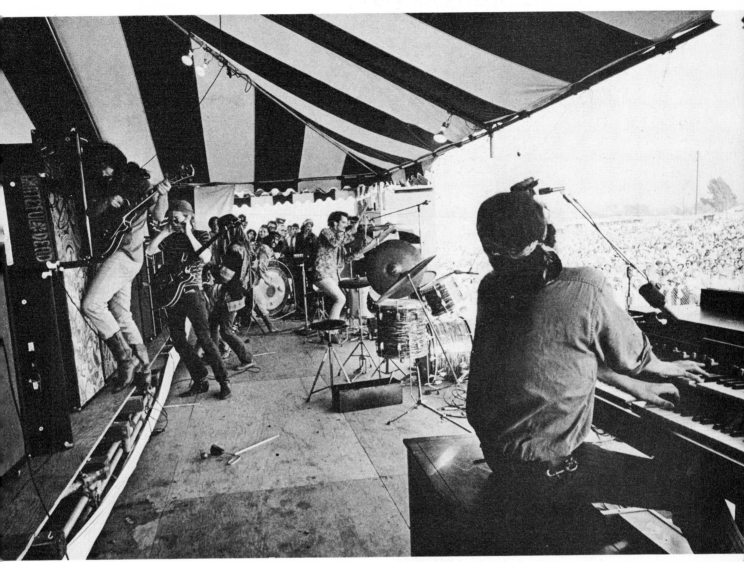

Feedback! Newport Pop Festival, Costa Mesa, California, August, 1968. Photo by Jim Marshall.

A moment of instinct is worth a lifetime of experience.

LIKE I TOLD YOU, WHAT I SAID
STEAL YOUR FACE
RIGHT OFF YOUR HEAD

we dance and dance
our bodies following as if by rote
instinctive, primitive commands

NOTHIN' LEFT TO DO
BUT SMILE SMILE SMILE

heads nod softly in agreement

LIKE A STEAM LOCOMOTIVE
ROLLIN' DOWN THE TRACK

the dirge unfolds
magnificently, as at a wake
so many names come to mind
Bobby Sands, John Lennon

Bob Marley
Hendrix   Janis   Pigpen

HE'S GONE, OHHHHHHNNNNNN
AND NOTHIN'S
GONNA BRING HIM BACK
HE'S GONE

but there's renewal too
and always hope
the amps flicker quietly
a natural pause for retuning
all systems apparently
go

"TRUCKIN'"

gaily bounding notes ring out
enthusiastically received

TRUCKIN'
GOT MY CHIPS CASHED IN

the oft-told couplets
sung out with obvious gusto
our response is electric
the body-rushes nearly tackle us all
and we rocket away again
a million metaphors
for what we're feeling
cognitive and meditative goo
smeared liberally about the cortex

SOMETIMES THE LIGHT'S
ALL SHINING ON ME
OTHER TIMES I CAN BARELY SEE

everyone knows
everyone shouts

LATELY IT OCCURS TO ME
WHAT A LONG
STRANGE TRIP IT'S BEEN

Jerry Garcia:

"Rhythmically, our policy is that the *one* is where you think it is. It's kind of a Zen concept, but it really works well for us. It makes it possible to get into a phrase where I can change into little phrase spurts, spitting out little groups of notes that are attached fives—five in the space of four, or five in the space of two is more common for me—and then turn that into a new pulse, where those fives become like a 16th-note pulse. Then I'm inside of a whole irregularly rotating tempo in relation to what the rest of the band is playing, when they're playing, say, the original common time. It produces this ambiguity, but all I have to do is make a statement that says, 'End of paragraph, AND, *one*,' and they all know where it is."

To David Gans and Blair Jackson
1981

Photo by Larry Hulst.

Photo by Dave Patrick.

yes, the legendary second set high
tripping my socks off
coming apart at the very seams
surrounded by 5,000 gonzo clowns
radiant, exulting
the famous story whistling by

BUSTED
DOWN ON BOURBON STREET

but this tale is just a matrix
a grid of electronic epigrams
and experiential human calculus
manytalk   grouprap   allgrok
the obvious not so obvious at all

GET OUT OF THE DOOR
LIGHT OUT AND LOOK AROUND

kapow!!

Lesh uncorks a mighty blast
we stand there, poleaxed
stupefied with pleasure

BACK HOME
SIT DOWN AND PATCH MY BONES
AND GET BACK TRUCKIN' ON

roll up your sleeves now
fast track for a distant border
tailpipes glowing red
our engines fire-stoked
we thunder down the tarmac
once aboard, there's no stopping
as notes careen past the windows
exploding into jagged shards
angry hornets of crystal shrapnel
bursting on our ears
Sinbad and crew lashed to the mast
at the mercy of a savage cyclone

no quarter asked or given
—there's no one at the helm!
the Dead Heads too must ride it out
Weir lunges forward
the drummers a pack of wild dogs
Garcia improvising recklessly
writhing and contorting
to the abyss and beyond he takes us
down down down
into a swollen, turbulent chasm
strangers and friends
indistinguishable in the
purple awfulness
destroying all credulity
befuddling our brains
shellshocked, we gasp in disbelief
but the band resolutely pushes on
to higher and firmer ground
the tension melts away
replaced by growing expectation
just what do you suppose is next?

into "ST. STEPHEN"

ah, the great boulders
comprising the foundation
of this roly-poly song
endlessly surging
cresting and breaking into
shimmery porcelain passages
like candy on the lips
you can taste the sweetness

**ONE MAN GATHERS
WHAT ANOTHER MAN SPILLS**

the Dead howl anew
sledgehammering against the rock
sparks flying
bam *badam*
bam *badam*
such heroics!
the fainthearted need not apply

**BUT WHAT WOULD
BE THE ANSWER
TO THE ANSWER MAN?**

there are no words for what we feel
we have entered a brave new galaxy
beyond all ken or comprehension
as if speechlessness were Esperanto
we're aware that anything can happen
here at the concert, frozen in time
by and by the jam trails off

leaving Mickey and Billy on stage
to share their thoughts with us

into "RHYTHM DEVILS"

garrulous, they talk of distant lands
the Hindu Kush, Mozambique
Egypt, the plains of Patagonia
all through the magic of their drums
slowly they move about The Beast
bringing forth the essence

of each instrument
intuitively they build momentum
and the power they find
shatters the air
swarms through the building
we are riveted in admiration
this is uniquely Grateful Dead
compelling and relentless
but achieved through different means
this is *soul*
born of naked rhythm and trust

it is almost beyond applause
quietly the other Dead edge back in
fitting threads to the tapestry
weaving a new spell
and the jam gains speed again
following the mysterious gyroscope
but without maps or signposts
an echo-y region is traversed
a brittle, metallic moonscape
full of monsters and apparitions
joining in an unearthly clamor

*The sound test did such amazing
things to my blown-out head I almost
forgot I was an oiled sardine.*

Dead Head letter
Atherton, California, 1974

broken by Phil's crack of doom
and almost without warning
we're at a major intersection

SPANISH LADY COME TO ME
SHE LAYS ON ME THIS ROSE

into "THE OTHER ONE"

halfway to Saturn we've traveled
in star-drive acceleration
and yet our position is familiar

COMIN' COMIN' COMIN' AROUND

Lesh rips at the theme
lighting fuses, detonating charges
Garcia in feverish pursuit
tunneling through the smoke
blasting into ozone atoms
then Weir steps forward
as if in a dream

THE BUS CAME BY AND I GOT ON
THAT'S WHEN IT ALL BEGAN

it doesn't matter *how* you get there
if you don't know *where* you're going

COWBOY NEAL AT THE WHEEL
OF THE BUS TO NEVER EVER LAND

we all combine in recognition

COMIN' COMIN' COMIN' AROUND

and now it's *On Beyond Zebra*
a click of the universal switch
entering a real screamer of a jam
a devastating danse macabre
springing from the acid bowels
shrieking, moaning, possessed
by every demon imaginable
until there's nothing left of us
just the Dead and the Dead Heads

dripping in our own blood
hearts pounding, chests heaving
a hellish three-ring circus
at the outer fringes of reality
only Garcia can pull us through

into "WHARF RAT"

rudderless, we drift in the current
the passion play intensifies

OLD MAN DOWN
WAY DOWN DOWN
DOWN BY THE DOCKS
OF THE CITY

the bluest introspection
stage and band bathed in shadow
Garcia sings for everyone tonight
slowly, ever slowly building
awesomely, achingly human
wringing torrents of emotion

from each and every brow

**I KNOW THAT THE LIFE
I'M LIVING'S NO GOOD**

where there were cheers
there is now only the deepest
and most profound silence

**I'LL GET A NEW START
LIVE THE LIFE I SHOULD**

everything is at a dead stop
time hangs in the balance

**I'LL GET UP AND FLY AWAY
FLY AWAY**

and then he concentrates *hard*
audacious and unabashed
every sinew focused on the solo
the night's deepest penetration
spiraling in tortuously, angrily

violating all our senses
we surrender to his vision
swallowed whole, devoured
and amidst tears of joy and pain
ultimately resurrected

into "SUGAR MAGNOLIA"

embraced in joy and exultation
we're a total dance once more
energy ricocheting off the roof
the floor a sweating shambles
every man, woman, and child
possessed by pure and holy pleasure

**SHE CAN DANCE A CAJUN RHYTHM
JUMP LIKE A WILLYS
IN 4-WHEEL DRIVE**

clapping, stomping, carrying on
a blitzkrieg of excitement
total rock and roll
Weir and the Dead hump and pump
till they move the balcony

and fuckin' *tear* the house down

into "SUNSHINE DAYDREAM"

*boom! like a nitromethane firestorm
boom ba-boom!!*—it *cannot* be denied
it's the mother of it all
and it's the **Dead**, pure and simple
we dance like there is no tomorrow
rapturously content
truly, when this band is on
there's nothing else like it
and absolutely no holding back

understatement of the year—
the third set encores blew us away

"DARK STAR"
into "NOT FADE AWAY"
into "UNCLE JOHN'S BAND"
into "AND WE BID YOU GOODNIGHT"

and thank *you* for a real good time! ■

Photo © Snooky Flowers.

Photo by Jerilyn Brandelius.

Photo by Ed Perlstein.

Photo by Jim Marshall.

You're obviously very intrigued by percussion instruments from other cultures. Do you think about how the audience will react?

HART: If we like it, they'll like it; that's how we've always approached it. If we get off by it, we know that people listening will get off by it.

KREUTZMANN: A good example is this thing we did with Hamza El-Din Sunday night [August 5] at the Oakland Auditorium. The audience started clapping in the *most unusual* time.

HART: *I couldn't believe it!* That was great.

KREUTZMANN: It was just fantastic to hear them playing along.

[*Here, Hart grabs a tar and demonstrates the beat played on stage while Kreutzmann and Hurwitz clap the audience's 4/4 time participation.*]

KREUTZMANN: The audience was a percussion instrument. We were using them as part of the solo!

HART: There was a time we played with Hamza, and the audience clapped a complicated twelve-beat pattern with us. Twelve beats! I wouldn't have thought it possible.

KREUTZMANN: Maybe our audience listens more than other audiences.

HART [*in hushed tones*]: You know, it's magic when you can bring five thousand people down to just your finger, and then build it back up from a whisper to a scream.

KREUTZMANN: Traditionally, drum solos always had to be just full bore blown-out events.

HART: But we don't go for the applause. We build on that sketch, we walk out on that landscape just trying to see what it feels like that night. It's one of the things I appreciate most, personally.

Miles Hurwitz
BAM, August 17, 1979

They went off into spaces I hadn't ever imagined existed.

A Dead Head from the word drop.

Dead Head letter
Harrisburg, Pennsylvania, 1979

Can we make earth heaven if we just get high enough?
Dead Head letter
1980

Did you know you have such a capacity for joy?

Alice Polesky, Changes, June 15, 1970

Our cheers were wet with our tears as we realized they were leaving the stage.

Rick Cohen
Fusion, *February, 1970*

Photo by Chuck Pulin.

"And They Played St. Stephen" by an unknown artist. ▶

The crowd, as always, went mildly berserk at every opportunity, throwing their hands into the air like thousands of tiny shrimp waggling in a wading pool.

John L. Wasserman
San Francisco Chronicle, *October 11, 1972*

When the Dead are playing their best, blood drips from the ceiling in great, rich drops. Together we do a kind of suicide in music.

Robert Hunter
Crawdaddy, *January, 1975*

The band built to an excruciating climax, and then caught its breath to build to another, and another; wave after wave, crescendo after crescendo.

Mike DeLong
Colorado Springs (Colorado) Sun, *April 30, 1970*

Photo by Ed Perlstein.

Before the Dead's encore at the Warfield, a table
with glasses of champagne was set up on stage.
Unknown to the band, Graham's workers also
passed out champagne to the crowd, knowing
the fans wouldn't toss the bubbly around.

The band came out and raised its glasses for a
toast. Suddenly, Graham flipped the switch on
special London air-raid lights that revealed the
crowd of 2,200 toasting the band. A garland
of roses hung from the balcony reading,
"Thank You!"

Mark Whittington
The (San Rafael, California) Independent-Journal, *October 25, 1980*

Homeward Bound

Thanks for gently taking away my
musical virginity and replacing it
with a cosmic orgasm.
Dead Head letter
Atlanta, Georgia, 1977

Dear BAM,

Just got back from seeing the Dead at the Warfield. We had front row seats for two-thirds of the best show I've ever experienced. I knew it was too good to last. The concert was so *intense* and *excellent* that my good friend Henry lost all control of his senses. We had to carry him away before the third set (too high). Our seats probably went to a good cause. Henry was so out of it he left muttering, "Where do I meet Jerry?" and "Was it real?" I just want to thank the whole band for one hot shit show. "Lazy Lightning" blew me away.

Bubs V.
Arcata
Letter to the editor
BAM, *October 17, 1980*

WHY DEAD CONCERTS ARE LIKE A CAUCUS-RACE.

"What *is* a Caucus-race?" said Alice.

"Why," said the Dodo, "the best way to explain it is to do it."

First it marked out a race course, in a sort of circle ("the exact shape doesn't matter," it said), and then all the party was placed along the course, here and there. There was no "One, two, three, and away!" but they began running when they liked and left off when they liked, so that it was not easy to know when the race was over. However, when they had been running half an hour or so, the Dodo suddenly called out, "The race is over!" and they all crowded round it, panting, and asking, "But who has won?"

This question the Dodo could not answer without a great deal of thought. At last the Dodo said, "*Everybody* has won, and *all* must have prizes."

Peter Wing
From Alice's Adventure in Wonderland *by Lewis Carroll*

Photo by Richard McCaffrey

I was at the Grateful Dead
We all got the munchies
And we all got fed.
Dead Head letter
1973

Photo by Chuck Pulin

Photo by Jim Marshall.

It was a very hot night, standing outside I noticed a weird guy walking toward me. OH G-D, Phil Lesh approaches. I was very wasted, so was he. I tried to start a conversation with him. "Hey, you know you look familiar?" I said. He looked at me, smiled and said, "So Do You." I was freakin' out. He had a brown paper bag in his hand. I asked, "What's in the bag?" He reached slowly into the bag—he was acting really weird. I was really wrecked. He suddenly pulled his hand out of the bag...I jumped back about 5 feet. In the hand was an ice cold can of beer. He gave it to me and then he split. He left me standing there holding the can. I kept saying to myself, "That didn't happen, did it?" All the way to Canarsie. By the way, I still have the can.

Cliff Goldfarb
Relix, *January-February, 1977*

Illustration by Pat Shen Yoshitsu.

Somehow, we float outside and dead-reckon our way to the bus. One after another, all 10 of us find our way, count noses, and start home. Luckily, there's a Dead tape to plug in.

A sleepily spaced slide back down the pike finds us at the close of One More Saturday Night. The driver, good ole Morris, deserves and wins a round of applause from us all for nifty navigation. We're grateful, but like him, dead tired.

Hugh Cutler
(Wilmington, Delaware) Evening Journal
March 30, 1972

Photo by Mary Ann Mayer. ▶

Turn on your
love light...
and leave it on!

Encore

Grateful Dead Tour List

1961

May 5   Peninsula School, Menlo Park, California [Jerry Garcia, Robert Hunter]

May   Arroyo Room, Stanford University, Palo Alto, California [Garcia, Hunter]

June-August   Boar's Head, San Carlos, California [Garcia, Hunter, Ron (Pigpen) McKernan, in various combinations]

1962

January-December   Boar's Head, Jewish Community Center, Belmont, California [Garcia, Hunter, Ken Frankel, Jim and Joe Edmiston, David Nelson, Norm Van Maastricht, in various combinations]

February   KPFA-FM studios, Berkeley, California [Garcia]

May 11   Stanford University, Palo Alto, California—folk festival [Thunder Mountain Tub Thumpers: Garcia, Hunter, Frankel, Edmistons]

June   Monterey County, California—sheriff's campaign party [Hart Valley Drifters: Garcia, Hunter, Frankel, Edmistons]

November 10   Art gallery, San Francisco State College, San Francisco, California [Hart Valley Drifters: Garcia, Hunter, Nelson, Van Maastricht]

November 10   College of San Mateo, Burlingame, California—folk festival [Hart Valley Drifters: Garcia, Hunter, Nelson, Van Maastricht]

1963

February 22   Top of the Tangent, Palo Alto, California [Wildwood Boys: Garcia, Hunter, Nelson]

Spring   Top of the Tangent, Palo Alto, California [Jerry and Sara: Garcia, Sara Garcia]

May   Fairgrounds, Monterey, California—Monterey Folk Festival [Wildwood Boys: Garcia, Hunter, Nelson, Frankel]

May   San Francisco State College, San Francisco, California—folk festival [Wildwood Boys: Garcia, Hunter, Nelson, Frankel]

August   Top of the Tangent, Palo Alto, California [Wildwood Boys: Garcia, Nelson, Frankel]

August   Coffee Gallery, San Francisco, California [Wildwood Boys: Garcia, Nelson, Frankel]

December [around Christmas]   The Ashgrove, Los Angeles, California [Bad Water Valley Boys: Garcia, Hunter, Frankel, Marshall Leicester]

1964

March   Cabale Creamery, Berkeley, California [Garcia, Hunter, Nelson, Austin Keith]

March 6, 7   Top of the Tangent, Palo Alto, California [Black Mountain Boys: Garcia, Hunter, Sandy Rothman, Eric Thompson, Peter Albin]

May 1, 2   Top of the Tangent, Palo Alto, California [Mother McCree's Uptown Jug Champions: Garcia, Weir, Pigpen, David Parker, Bob Matthews, John Dawson, and others]

May   San Francisco State College, San Francisco, California—folk festival [Mother McCree's Uptown Jug Champions]

May 21, 23, 29, 30   Mime Troupe loft, San Francisco, California—The New Music [various performers, pieces composed by Phil Lesh, Tom Constanten, and others]

July 16-18   Top of the Tangent, Palo Alto, California [Mother McCree's Uptown Jug Champions]

August 28   Magoo's Pizza Parlor, Menlo Park, California [Mother McCree's Uptown Jug Champions]

August or December   The Offstage, San Jose, California [Redwood Canyon Ramblers: Garcia, Rothman, Scott Hambley]

1965

January   College of San Mateo, Burlingame, California [Mother McCree's Uptown Jug Champions]

Garcia, Weir, Pigpen, Bill Kreutzmann, and Dana Morgan form the Warlocks.

(April)   Menlo College, Menlo Park, California

May 5, (12), 27   Magoo's Pizza Parlor, Menlo Park, California

Phil Lesh joins the Warlocks at the Frenchy's gig.

June or July   Frenchy's, Fremont, California [gig cancelled after one night]

August [possibly three nights]   Fireside Club, San Mateo, California

August   Big Al's, Redwood City, California

August   Cinnamon a Go Go, Redwood City, California

September-November [six weeks, four to six nights a week]   The In Room, Belmont, California

November 3   San Francisco, California—Autumn Records demo recording

November [possibly three nights]   Pierre's, San Francisco, California

The Warlocks become the Grateful Dead—Garcia, Weir, Pigpen, Kreutzmann, Lesh.

December 4   Big Nig's house, San Jose, California—Acid Test

December 10   Fillmore Auditorium, San Francisco, California—Mime Troupe benefit

December 11   Muir Beach Lodge, Muir Beach, California—Acid Test

December 18   Big Beat Club, Palo Alto, California—Acid Test

December [between Christmas and New Year's]   Matrix, San Francisco, California

1966

January   Portland, Oregon—Acid Test

January 7, (8)   Matrix, San Francisco, California

January 8   Fillmore Auditorium, San Francisco, California—Acid Test

January 14   Fillmore Auditorium, San Francisco, California—Mime Troupe benefit

January 15, 16   Matrix, San Francisco, California

January 22, 23   Longshoremen's Hall, San Francisco, California—Trips Festival, second and third nights

January 28, 29   Matrix, San Francisco, California

January 29   Sound City Studios, San Francisco, California—Acid Test

February 10   Cabale Creamery, Berkeley, California

February 11   Youth Opportunities Center, Compton, California—Watts Acid Test

February   (San Fernando Valley Unitarian Church), Northridge, California

February   Los Angeles, California—Sunset Acid Test

February   (Danish Hall), Los Angeles, California

March (25)   (Troopers Hall), Los Angeles, California

April (5)   Los Angeles, California—Pico Acid Test

April 22-24   Longshoremen's Hall, San Francisco, California—Trips '6? Festival

The band summers at Rancho Olompali and Camp Lagunitas, Marin County, California, April through August.

May 14   Veteran's Hall, Berkeley, California

May 19   Avalon Ballroom, San Francisco, California [Straight Theater production]

May 27-29   Avalon Ballroom, San Francisco, California [first Family Dog production with Grateful Dead on bill]

May 29   California Hall, San Francisco, California—legalize marijuana benefit

June 3, 4   Fillmore Auditorium, San Francisco, California

June 10, 11   Avalon Ballroom, San Francisco, California

June 17, 18   Veteran's Hall, San Jose, California

June   University of California Medical Center, San Francisco, California—LSD conference

June or July   Pauley Ballroom, University of California, Berkeley, California

June or July   Winterland, San Francisco, California

June, July, August [numerous unscheduled performances]   Speedway Meadows and Panhandle, Golden Gate Park, San Francisco, California

July 3   Fillmore Auditorium, San Francisco, California

July 14   Fillmore Auditorium, San Francisco, California—A Pleasure Dome

July 15-17   Fillmore Auditorium, San Francisco, California

July 30   Vancouver, Canada—British Columbia Festival

August 5, 6   Afterthought, Vancouver, Canada

August 7   Fillmore Auditorium, San Francisco, California—Children's Adventure Day Camp benefit

August 12, 13, 19, 20   Avalon Ballroom, San Francisco, California [possibly Fillmore Auditorium, 12 and 13]

"Stealin' " and "Don't Ease Me In" recorded for Scorpio Records, but the single is not released.

August 27, 28   Grange Hall, Pescadero, California—bike race weekend

The Dead take up residence at 710 Ashbury Street, San Francisco, where they will live, more or less communally, through March, 1968.

September 2   La Dolphine, Hillsborough, California—debutante dance

September (3), 4, (5)   Fillmore Auditorium, San Francisco, California [first headline date produced by Bill Graham]

September 5   Rancho Olompali, Novato, California

September 11   Fillmore Auditorium, San Francisco, California—Both/And Club benefit

September 16, 17   Avalon Ballroom, San Francisco, California [first Kelley/Mouse use of skull and roses motif in Dead's poster art]

October 2   Cafeteria, San Francisco State University, San Francisco, California—Acid Test

October 6   Golden Gate Park, San Francisco, California—LSD rally

October 7, 8   Winterland, San Francisco, California

October 8   Mt. Tamalpais Amphitheater, Marin County, California—Peace Festival

October 9   Fillmore Auditorium, San Francisco, California

October 9 or 12   Golden Gate Park, San Francisco, California—Artists Liberation Front Free Festival

October 15   The Heliport, Novato, California

October 16   Rancho Olompali, Novato, California—Sunday Party

October 21, 22   Fillmore Auditorium, San Francisco, California

October 26   The North Face ski shop, San Francisco, California

October 31   California Hall, San Francisco, California [same night as Ken Kesey's Acid Test Graduation]

October or November   Student Union, Stanford University, Palo Alto, California

November 4, 5   Avalon Ballroom, San Francisco, California

November 12   Old Cheese Factory, San Francisco, California

November 13   Avalon Ballroom, San Francisco, California—Zen Center benefit

November 18, 19   Fillmore Auditorium, San Francisco, California

November 20   Fillmore Auditorium, San Francisco, California—Student Nonviolent Coordinating Committee benefit

November 23   Fillmore Auditorium, San Francisco, California—private Thanksgiving party

December 2   Pauley Ballroom, University of California, Berkeley, California—Danse Macabre

December 9-11, 20, (21)   Fillmore Auditorium, San Francisco, California

December 23, 24   Avalon Ballroom, San Francisco, California

December 28   Governor's Hall, Sacramento, California—Beaux Arts Ball

December 29   Santa Venetia Armory, Marin City, California

December 30, 31   Fillmore Auditorium, San Francisco, California [first Bill Graham-produced New Year's concert, 31]

1967

January 1   Panhandle, Golden Gate Park, San Francisco, California—Hells Angels-sponsored thank-you dance for Diggers

January 13-15   Fillmore Auditorium, San Francisco, California

The band begins recording their first album, *Grateful Dead.*

January 14   Golden Gate Park, San Francisco, California—Human Be-In

January 27, 28   Avalon Ballroom, San Francisco, California

January 29   Avalon Ballroom, San Francisco, California—Krishna Consciousness Comes West

February 12   Fillmore Auditorium, San Francisco, California—CCU benefit

February 24-26   Fillmore Auditorium, San Francisco, California

March 3   Winterland, San Francisco, California—First Annual Love Circus

Grateful Dead is released, March 17.

March 17-19   Fillmore Auditorium, San Francisco, California [possibly Winterland, 17 and 18]

March 20   Fugazi Hall, San Francisco, California—album release party

March 24, 25   Avalon Ballroom, San Francisco, California

April 12   Fillmore Auditorium, San Francisco, California—Mime Troupe benefit

April   Continental Ballroom, Santa Clara, California

April 29   Earl Warren Fairgrounds, Santa Barbara, California

May 5, 6   Fillmore Auditorium, San Francisco, California

May 30   Winterland, San Francisco, California—Haight-Ashbury Legal Organization benefit

May-June [every Monday night]   Rendezvous Inn, San Francisco, California

June 6-11   Cafe A Go Go, New York, New York

June 8   Bandshell on the mall, Central Park, New York, New York

June 12   The Cheetah, New York, New York

June   Tompkins Square Park, New York, New York

June 15   Mt. Tamalpais Amphitheater, Marin County, California—Magic Mountain Music Festival

June 15   Straight Theater, San Francisco, California—Christening

June   El Camino Park, Palo Alto, California

June 18   Fairgrounds, Monterey, California—Monterey International Pop Festival

June 21   Golden Gate Park, San Francisco, California—Summer Solstice Festival

June 28   Oakland Auditorium, Oakland, California

July (4)   Hitchcock Mansion, Millbrook, New York [Timothy Leary's headquarters]

July 13   Pacific National Exhibition Agrodome, Vancouver, Canada

(July   Portland, Oregon)

July (16), 23   Straight Theater, San Francisco, California—grand opening, 23

July 31-August 5   O'Keefe Center, Toronto, Canada [matinee performance, 2 and 5]

August   Montreal, Canada—Expo '67

August 13   West Park, Ann Arbor, Michigan

August   American Legion Hall, South Shore, Lake Tahoe, Nevada

August 28   Lindley Meadow, Golden Gate Park, San Francisco, California—Chocolate George's funeral

September 2   Palace of Fine Arts, San Francisco, California

September (4) [Labor Day weekend]   Rio Nido, California

September   Continental Ballroom, Santa Clara, California

September 15   Hollywood Bowl, Los Angeles, California

September 22, 23   Family Dog, Denver, Colorado

Mickey Hart plays in concert with the Dead for the first time, September 29.

September 29, 30   Straight Theater, San Francisco, California—dance lessons

The Dead's house at 710 Ashbury Street, San Francisco, is busted, October 2.

(**October**   Matrix, San Francisco, California)

October 21 or 31   Winterland, San Francisco, California—Marijuana Defense benefit

The band begins recording *Anthem of the Sun*.

November 8-11   Shrine Auditorium, Los Angeles, California

December 13   (Shrine Auditorium, Los Angeles, California)

December 23, 24   Palm Gardens, New York, New York

December 26, 27   Second Avenue Theater, aka Village Theater, New York, New York [theater later named Fillmore East by Bill Graham]

December [possibly two nights]   Boston, Massachusetts

1968

The Dead and the Jefferson Airplane begin to manage the Carousel Ballroom in San Francisco, January.

January 17   Carousel Ballroom, San Francisco, California

January 20   Eureka, California–Great Northwest Tour begins

January 22, 26, 27   Eagles Auditorium, Seattle, Washington

January 29   Portland State College, Portland, Oregon

February 2, 3   Crystal Ballroom, Portland, Oregon

February 4   Gym, South Oregon College, Ashland, Oregon

February (7)   Avalon Ballroom, San Francisco, California

February 14   Carousel Ballroom, San Francisco, California—official opening

February 22-24   The Bowl, King's Beach, Lake Tahoe, Nevada

March 3   Haight Street, San Francisco, California

March 7   Avalon Ballroom, San Francisco, California

March 15-17   Carousel Ballroom, San Francisco, California

March 20   Avalon Ballroom, San Francisco, California—KMPX-FM strike benefit

March 26   location unknown

March 29-31   Carousel Ballroom, San Francisco, California

April 3   Winterland, San Francisco, California—KMPX-FM strike benefit

April 19   Avalon Ballroom, San Francisco, California

May 1 or 2 or 3   Student Union roof, Columbia University, New York, New York

May 4   State University of New York, Stony Brook, New York

May 5   Central Park, New York, New York

May 7-9   Electric Circus, New York, New York

May 18   Santa Clara County Fairgrounds, San Jose, California—Northern California Folk-Rock Festival

May 30-June 1   Carousel Ballroom, San Francisco, California

June 6   Avalon Ballroom, San Francisco, California

June 7-9   Carousel Ballroom, San Francisco, California

June (10, 11), 12, 13   Paradise Theater, aka Paramount Theater, Staten Island, New York—Daytop Village Drug Rehabilitation Center benefit

June 14, 15   Fillmore East, New York, New York

Anthem of the Sun is released, July 18.

August 2, 3   Hippodrome, San Diego, California

August 4 or 5   Costa Mesa, California—Newport Pop Festival

The Carousel Ballroom folds; Bill Graham reopens it as Fillmore West.

August (16-18), 20-22   Fillmore West, San Francisco, California

August 23, 24   Shrine Auditorium, Los Angeles, California

August 30-September 1   Fillmore West, San Francisco, California

September 2   Betty Nelson's organic raspberry farm, Sultan, Washington—Sky River Festival

The Dead begin recording *Aoxomoxoa*, September 5.

September 22   Del Mar Race Track, San Diego, California

October 8, 10   Matrix, San Francisco, California [as Mickey Hart and the Heartbeats]

October 11-13   Avalon Ballroom, San Francisco, California

October 19   Matrix, San Francisco, California [as Mickey Hart and the Heartbeats]

October 20   Greek Theater, University of California, Berkeley, California

October 21   (Jefferson Airplane House), San Francisco, California

October 22   Avalon Ballroom, San Francisco, California

October 29-31   Matrix, San Francisco, California [as Mickey Hart and the Heartbeats]

November 7-10   Fillmore West, San Francisco, California

November   (Omaha, Nebraska)

November 22   Ohio State University, Columbus, Ohio

Tom Constanten plays in concert with the Dead for the first time, November 23.

November 23   Legion Hall, Athens, Ohio

December 1   Grand Ballroom, Detroit, Michigan

December 16   Matrix, San Francisco, California [as Mickey Hart and the Heartbeats]

December 24   Matrix, San Francisco, California [as Jerry Garcia and Friends]

December 31   Winterland, San Francisco, California

1969

January 2-4   Fillmore West, San Francisco, California

January 24-26   Avalon Ballroom, San Francisco, California

February 5   location unknown

February 11, 12   Fillmore East, New York, New York

February 14, 15   Electric Theater, Philadelphia, Pennsylvania

February 19   Fillmore West, San Francisco, California—Celestial Synapse

February 22   Dream Bowl, Napa, California

February 27-March 2   Fillmore West, San Francisco, California

March 15   Hilton Hotel, San Francisco, California—Black and White Ball

March 21, 22   Rose Palace, Pasadena, California

March 28   Modesto, California

The Dead begin recording *Live Dead*.

April 5, 6   Avalon Ballroom, San Francisco, California

April 12   Student Union Ballroom, University of Utah, Salt Lake City, Utah

April 13   Boulder, Colorado

April 17   Washington University, St. Louis, Missouri

April 18   Purdue University, West Lafayette, Indiana

April 21-23   The Ark, Boston, Massachusetts

April 25, 26   Electric Theater, Chicago, Illinois [possibly Aragon Ballroom]

April 27   (Labor Temple), Minneapolis, Minnesota

May 2, 3   Winterland, San Francisco, California

May 8   Golden Gate Park, San Francisco, California

May 9   San Mateo County Fairgrounds, Redwood City, California

May 10   Rose Palace, Pasadena, California

May 16   Campolindo High School, Moraga, California

May 23, 24   Hollywood, Florida—Big Rock Pow Wow

May 28   Winterland, San Francisco, California—People's Park benefit

May 29   Robertson Gym, University of California, Santa Barbara, California

May 30   Springer's Ballroom, Portland, Oregon

May 31   Eugene, Oregon

June 5-8   Fillmore West, San Francisco, California

June 20, 21   Fillmore East, New York, New York

Aoxomoxoa is released, June 20.

June 22   Central Park, New York, New York

June 27, 28   Santa Rosa, California

July 12   Central Park, New York, New York—Schaefer Music Festival

July 12, 13   New York State Pavilion, Flushing, New York

July 25-27   Exhibit Hall, Honolulu, Hawaii

August 1-3   Family Dog at the Great Highway, San Francisco, California

August   Fillmore East, New York, New York

August 16   Woodstock Music and Art Fair, Bethel, New York

August 21   AquaTheater, Seattle, Washington

August 29, 30   Family Dog at the Great Highway, San Francisco, California

September 1   Prairieville, Louisiana—New Orleans Pop Festival

September 7   Family Dog at the Great Highway, San Francisco, California

September 26, 27   Fillmore East, New York, New York

October 2-4   Boston Tea Party, Boston, Massachusetts

October 6   Family Dog at the Great Highway, San Francisco, California

October 24, 25, (26)   Winterland, San Francisco, California

November 2   Family Dog at the Great Highway, San Francisco, California

November 4   (Fillmore West), San Francisco, California

November 7, 8   Fillmore Auditorium, San Francisco, California

November 15   Lanai Theater, Crockett, California—Moratorium Day

November 21   Building A, Sacramento, California—Cal Expo

December 4-7   Fillmore West, San Francisco, California

December   Kaleidoscope, Los Angeles, California

December 10-12   Thelma Theater, Los Angeles, California

December 13   San Bernardino, California

December 19-21   Fillmore Auditorium, San Francisco, California

December 26   McFarlin Auditorium, Southern Methodist University, Dallas, Texas

December 28   Hollywood Pop Festival, Miami, Florida

December 30, 31   Boston Tea Party, Boston, Massachusetts

1970

January 2, 3   Fillmore East, New York, New York

Live Dead is released.

January 10   Community Concourse, San Diego, California

January 16, 18   Springer's Ballroom, Portland, Oregon

January 17   Oregon State University, Corvallis, Oregon

January 22-26   Civic Auditorium, Honolulu, Hawaii

January 30-February 1   The Warehouse, New Orleans, Louisiana

New Orleans police bust the Dead, January 31

February 2   Fox Theater, St. Louis, Missouri

February 4   Family Dog at the Great Highway, San Francisco, California [filmed for public television]

February 5-8   Fillmore West, San Francisco, California

February 10, 11, 13, 14   Fillmore East, New York, New York [*Bear's Choice* recorded]

February 20   Panther Hall, Fort Worth, Texas

February 21   Civic Center Arena, San Antonio, Texas

February 22   Sam Houston Coliseum, Houston, Texas

Jefferson Airplane, Quicksilver Messenger Service, Santana, It's a Beautiful Day, and Dan Hicks and His Hot Licks perform in a benefit to help defray the Dead's New Orleans bust expenses, February 23.

February 27-March 1   Family Dog at the Great Highway, San Francisco, California

The Dead begin recording *Workingman's Dead.*

March 7, (9, 10)   Star Theater, Phoenix, Arzonia

March 8   Civic Auditorium, Santa Monica, California

(March 10   Capitol Theater, Port Chester, Long Island, New York)

March 16   Kleinhaus Music Hall, Buffalo, New York

March 18, 19, (20, 21)   Capitol Theater, Port Chester, Long Island, New York

March 24   Pirate's World, Dania, Florida

April 3   Field House, University of Cincinnati, Cincinnati, Ohio

April 9-12   Fillmore West, San Francisco, California

April 15   Winterland, San Francisco, California

April 24, 25   Mammoth Gardens, Denver, Colorado

April 26   York Farm, Poynette, Wisconsin—Sound Storm Festival

May 1   Alfred College, Alfred, New York [with New Riders of the Purple Sage]

May 2   State University of New York, Harper College, Binghamton, New York [with NRPS]

May 3   Field House, Wesleyan University, Middletown, Connecticut [with NRPS]

May 6 or 7   Student Union steps, Massachusetts Institute of Technology, Cambridge, Massachusetts [with NRPS]

May 7   Massachusetts Institute of Technology, Cambridge, Massachusetts [with NRPS]

May 8   Farrell Hall, State University of New York, Delhi, New York [with NRPS]

May 9   Worcester Polytechnic Institute, Worcester, Massachusetts [with NRPS]

May 10   Sports Arena, Atlanta, Georgia

May 15   Merimec Community College, Kirkwood, Missouri [with NRPS]

May 16   Temple University, Philadelphia, Pennsylvania

May 17   Fairfield University, Fairfield, Connecticut

May 19   Washington University, St. Louis, Missouri [with NRPS]

May 24, (25)   Newcastle-under-Lyme, England—Hollywood Festival

May   The Roundhouse, London, England [possibly a rehearsal]

May 28   The Lyceum, London, England

June 4-7   Fillmore West, San Francisco, California [with NRPS]

June 12, 13   Civic Auditorium, Honolulu, Hawaii

June 19   Mid-South Coliseum, Memphis, Tennessee

June 21   Pauley Ballroom, University of California, Berkeley, California—American Indian benefit

June 24, 25   Capitol Theater, Port Chester, New York [with NRPS]

June 27   Canadian National Exhibition Hall, Toronto, Canada [with NRPS]

July 1   Fairgrounds, Winnipeg, Canada—Red River Exhibition [with NRPS]

July 5   McMahon Stadium, Calgary, Canada [with NRPS]

July 8   Edwardsville, Illinois—Mississippi River Festival

July 9-12   Fillmore East, New York, New York

July 14   Euphoria, San Rafael, California [with NRPS]

July 30   (Matrix), San Francisco, California

August 5   Community Concourse, San Diego, California

August 17-19   Fillmore West, San Francisco, California [with NRPS]

August 28, 29   The Club, Los Angeles, California [with NRPS]

August 30   San Francisco, California—Calibration

The Dead begin recording *American Beauty.*

September 13   University of Rochester, Rochester, New York

September 17-20   Fillmore East, New York, New York

September 25   Civic Auditorium, Pasadena, California

September 26   Terrace Ballroom, Salt Lake City, Utah

October 3, 4   Winterland, San Francisco, California [first quadraphonic radio and TV broadcast]

October 10, 11   (Paterson, New Jersey) [with NRPS]

October 16   Auditorium, Drexel University, Philadelphia, Pennsylvania [with NRPS]

October 17   The Music Hall, Cleveland, Ohio [with NRPS]

October 18   Northrup Auditorium, University of Minnesota, Minneapolis, Minnesota [with NRPS]

October 23   McDonough Arena, Georgetown University, Washington D.C. [with NRPS]

October 24   Kiel Auditorium, St. Louis, Missouri [with NRPS]

October 30, 31   State University of New York, Stony Brook, New York [with NRPS]

November 4-8   Capitol Theater, Port Chester, New York [with NRPS]

November 11   Action House, (Queens), New York [with NRPS]

November 12-14   46th Street Rock Palace, Brooklyn, New York [with NRPS]

November 16   Fillmore East, New York, New York [with NRPS]

November 20   The Palestra, University of Rochester, Rochester, New York [with NRPS]

November 21   Sargent Gym, Boston University, Boston, Massachusetts [with NRPS]

November 22   Middlesex Community College, Edison, New Jersey [with NRPS]

November 23   Anderson Theater, New York, New York [Hells Angels-sponsored concert, with NRPS]

American Beauty is released.

November 27   The Syndrome, Chicago, Illinois

November 29   Club Agora, Columbus, Ohio

December (10)   University of California, Davis, California

December 12   Sonoma County Fairgrounds, Santa Rosa, California [with NRPS]

December 22   Memorial Auditorium, Sacramento, California [with NRPS]

December 23   Winterland, San Francisco, California—benefit for "Bear"

December 26-28   Legion Stadium, El Monte, California [with NRPS]

December 31   Winterland, San Francisco, California [second quadraphonic radio and TV broadcast, with NRPS]

1971

January 19, 20 (possibly 1972)   Marin County Veterans Auditorium, San Rafael, California [with NRPS]

January 21   University of California, Davis, California [with NRPS]

January 22   Lane Community College, Eugene, Oregon [with NRPS]

January 23   Coliseum, Vancouver, Canada [with NRPS]

January 24   Arena, Seattle, Washington [with NRPS]

February 18-20, 22-24   Capitol Theater, Port Chester, New York [with NRPS]

March 3   Fillmore West, San Francisco, California—Airwaves Benefit

March 5   Auditorium, Oakland, California—Black Panther benefit

March 13   Michigan State University, Lansing, Michigan [with NRPS]

March 14   Madison, Wisconsin [with NRPS]

March 17, 18   Fox Theater, St. Louis, Missouri [with NRPS]

March 19   The Syndrome, Chicago, Illinois [with NRPS]

March 20   Iowa City, Iowa [with NRPS]

March 21   Exposition Center, Milwaukee, Wisconsin [with NRPS]

The Dead begin recording *Grateful Dead*.

March 24   Winterland, San Francisco, California—Sufi benefit [with NRPS]

April 4-6   Manhattan Center, New York, New York—Dance Marathon [with NRPS]

April 7, 8   The Music Hall, Boston, Massachusetts [with NRPS]

April 10   Franklin and Marshall University, Lancaster, Pennsylvania [with NRPS]

April 12   Civic Arena, Pittsburgh, Pennsylvania [with NRPS]

April 13   Youth Center, Scranton, Pennsylvania [with NRPS]

April 14   Bucknell University, Lewisburg, Pennsylvania [with NRPS]

April 15   Allegheny State College, Meadville, Pennsylvania [with NRPS]

April 17   Dillon Gym, Princeton University, Princeton, New Jersey [with NRPS]

April 18   State University of New York, Cortland, New York [with NRPS]

April 21   Rhode Island Auditorium, Providence, Rhode Island [with NRPS]

April 22   Municipal Auditorium, Bangor, Maine [with NRPS]

April 24   Duke University, Durham, North Carolina [with NRPS]

April 25-29   Fillmore East, New York, New York [with NRPS]

May 28-30   Winterland, San Francisco, California

Fillmore East closes.

June (21)   A chateau, Heronville, France

July 2   Fillmore West, San Francisco, California [with NRPS]

Fillmore West closes.

Jerry Garcia begins recording his first solo album.

July 31   Yale Bowl, Yale University, New Haven, Connecticut

August (3)   Terminal Island Correctional Facility, San Pedro, California—benefit for "Bear"

August 5, 6   Hollywood Palladium, Los Angeles, California [with NRPS]

August 7   Community Concourse, San Diego, California [with NRPS]

August 14, 15   Berkeley Community Theater, Berkeley, California [with NRPS]

August 23, 24   Auditorium Theater, Chicago, Illinois

August 26   Gaelic Park, Bronx, New York

First NRPS album, *New Riders of the Purple Sage,* released, September.

Grateful Dead live album released and Keith Godchaux joins band, October.

October 19   Northrup Auditorium, University of Minnesota, Minneapolis, Minnesota [with NRPS]

October 21, 22   Auditorium Theater, Chicago, Illinois [with NRPS]

October 23, 24   East Town Theater, Chicago, Illinois [with NRPS]

October 26   The Palestra, University of Rochester, Rochester, New York [with NRPS]

October 27   Onondaga County War Memorial Auditorium, Syracuse, New York [with NRPS]

October 29   Allen Theater, Cleveland, Ohio [with NRPS]

October 30   Taft Auditorium, Cincinnati, Ohio [with NRPS]

October 31   Ohio Theater, Columbus, Ohio [with NRPS]

Jerry Garcia and Howard Wales's *Hooteroll* album released.

November 6, 7   Harding Theater, San Francisco, California

November 11   The Auditorium, Atlanta, Georgia [with NRPS]

November 12   Auditorium, San Antonio, Texas [with NRPS]

November 14   Texas Christian University, Fort Worth, Texas [with NRPS]

November 15   Municipal Auditorium, Austin, Texas [with NRPS]

November 17   Civic Auditorium, Albuquerque, New Mexico [with NRPS]

November 20   Pauley Pavilion, University of California, Los Angeles, California

December 1, 2   The Music Hall, Boston, Massachusetts

December 4-7   Felt Forum, Madison Square Garden, New York, New York

December 9, 10   Fox Theater, St. Louis, Missouri

December 14, 15   Hill Auditorium, Ann Arbor, Michigan

December 31   Winterland, San Francisco, California

1972

January 2   Winterland, San Francisco, California

The Dead begin recording *Ace,* Bob Weir's "solo" album.

March 5   Winterland, San Francisco, California—American Indian benefit

Jerry Garcia's first solo album released.

Donna Godchaux joins band.

March (22), 23, 25-28   Academy of Music, New York, New York

The Dead begin recording *Europe '72.*

April 7, 8   Wembley Empire Pool, London, England

April 11   City Hall, Newcastle, England

April 14, 15   Tivoli Theater, Copenhagen, Denmark

April 16   Aarhus University, Aarhus, Denmark

April 17   Tivoli Gardens, Copenhagen, Denmark—TV from the Tivoli

April 21   Beat Club, Bremen, West Germany

April 24   Rheinhalle, Dusseldorf, West Germany

April 26   Jahrundert Halle, Frankfurt, West Germany

April 29   Musikhalle, Hamburg, West Germany

May 3, 4   Olympia Theater, Paris, France

May 7   Manchester, England—Bickershaw Festival

May 10   Concertgebouw, Amsterdam, The Netherlands

May 11   Civic Hall, Rotterdam, The Netherlands

May 13   Fairgrounds, Lille, France

May 16   Radio Luxembourg, Luxembourg

May 18   Deutsches Museum, Munich, West Germany

May 23-26   The Lyceum, London, England

Ace and Mickey Hart's *Rolling Thunder* released.

June 17   Hollywood Bowl, Los Angeles, California

July 16   Dillon Stadium, Hartford, Connecticut

July 18   Roosevelt Stadium, Jersey City, New Jersey

July 21, 22   Paramount Theater, Seattle, Washington

July 25, 26   Paramount Theater, Portland, Oregon

August 5   Hollywood Palladium, Los Angeles, California

August 12   Memorial Auditorium, Sacramento, California

August 20   Civic Auditorium, San Jose, California

August 21, 22, 24, 25   Berkeley Community Theater, Berkeley, California

August 28   Lane County Fairgrounds, Veneta, Oregon—Springfield Creamery benefit

September 3   Folsom Field, University of Colorado, Boulder, Colorado

September 9, 10   Hollywood Palladium, Los Angeles, California

September 15, 16   The Music Hall, Boston, Massachusetts

September 17   Civic Center, Baltimore, Maryland

September 19   Roosevelt Stadium, Jersey City, New Jersey

September 21   The Spectrum, Philadelphia, Pennsylvania

September 23, 24   The Palace Theater, Waterbury, Connecticut

September 26-28   Stanley Theater, Jersey City, New Jersey

September 30   American University, Washington, D.C.

October 2   Civic Center, Springfield, Massachusetts

October 9   Winterland, San Francisco, California—road crew benefit

October 17-19   Fox Theater, St. Louis, Missouri

October 21   Vanderbilt University, Nashville, Tennessee

October 23, 24   Performing Arts Center, Milwaukee, Wisconsin

October 26   Music Hall, Cincinnati, Ohio

October 27   Veterans Memorial Auditorium, Columbus, Ohio

October 28   Public Auditorium, Cleveland, Ohio

October 30   Ford Auditorium, Detroit, Michigan

Europe '72 is released.

November 12, 13   Kansas City, Missouri

November 14, 15   Music Hall, Oklahoma City, Oklahoma

November 17   Wichita, Kansas

November 18, 19   Hofheinz Pavilion, Houston, Texas

November 22, (23)   Municipal Auditorium, Austin, Texas

November 24   Memorial Auditorium, Dallas, Texas

November 26   Civic Auditorium, San Antonio, Texas

December 10-12   Winterland, San Francisco, California

December 15   Arena, Long Beach, California

December 31   Winterland, San Francisco, California

1973

February 9   Maples Pavilion, Stanford University, Palo Alto, California

February 15   Dane County Coliseum, Madison, Wisconsin

February 17   Auditorium, St. Paul, Minnesota

February 19   International Amphitheater, Chicago, Illinois

February 21, 22   Assembly Hall, University of Illinois, Champaign-Urbana, Illinois

February 24   Iowa State University, Iowa City, Iowa

February 26, 27   Pershing Municipal Auditorium, Lincoln, Nebraska

February 28   Salt Palace, Salt Lake City, Utah

Pigpen dies after a long illness, March.

March 15-17   Nassau Coliseum, Uniondale, New York

March 18   Felt Forum, Madison Square Garden, New York, New York [NRPS, including Garcia and Weir]

March 19   Nassau Coliseum, Uniondale, New York

March 21, 22   Municipal Auditorium, Utica, New York

March 24   The Spectrum, Philadelphia, Pennsylvania

March 26   Civic Center, Baltimore, Maryland

March 28   Civic Center, Springfield, Massachusetts

March 30   War Memorial Auditorium, Rochester, New York

March 31   War Memorial Auditorium, Buffalo, New York

April 1, (2)   Boston Garden, Boston, Massachusetts

May 13   State Fairgrounds, Des Moines, Iowa

May 20   Stadium, University of California, Santa Barbara, California

May 26   Kezar Stadium, San Francisco, California

June 2, (3)   Memorial Auditorium, Kansas City, Missouri

June 9, 10   Robert F. Kennedy Stadium, Washington, D.C.

Bear's Choice is released.

June 22   Pacific National Exhibition Coliseum, Vancouver, Canada

June 24   Coliseum, Portland, Oregon

June 26   Center Arena, Seattle, Washington

June 29-July 1   Universal Amphitheater, Universal City, California

July 20   Stadium, Duke University, Durham, North Carolina

July 27, 28   Grand Prix Racecourse, Watkins Glen, New York

July 31, August 1   Roosevelt Stadium, Jersey City, New Jersey

The Dead begin recording *Wake of the Flood*.

September 7-9   Nassau Coliseum, Uniondale, New York

September 11, 12   William and Mary College, Williamsburg, Virginia

September 14, 15   Civic Center, Providence, Rhode Island

September 17, 18   Onondaga War Memorial Auditorium, Syracuse, New York

September 20, 21   The Spectrum, Philadelphia, Pennsylvania

September 24   Civic Arena, Pittsburgh, Pennsylvania

September 26   War Memorial Auditorium, Buffalo, New York

Wake of the Flood is released, October 15.

October 19   Fairgrounds Arena, Oklahoma City, Oklahoma

October 21   Civic Auditorium, Omaha, Nebraska

October 23   Metropolitan Sports Center, Bloomington, Minnesota

October 25   Dane County Coliseum, Madison, Wisconsin

October 27   State Fair Coliseum, Indianapolis, Indiana

October 29, 30   Kiel Auditorium, St. Louis, Missouri

November 1   McGaw Memorial Hall, Northwestern University, Evanston, Illinois

November 9-11   Winterland, San Francisco, California

November 14   International Sports Arena, San Diego, California

November 17   Pauley Pavilion, University of California, Los Angeles, California

November 20, 21   Coliseum, Denver, Colorado

November 23   County Coliseum, El Paso, Texas

November 25   Sun Devil Stadium, University of Arizona, Tempe, Arizona

November 30-December 2   The Music Hall, Boston, Massachusetts

December 4   Cincinnati Gardens, Cincinnati, Ohio

December 6   Convention Center, Cleveland, Ohio

December 8   Cameron Indoor Stadium, Duke University, Durham, North Carolina

December 10   Memorial Coliseum, Charlotte, North Carolina

December 12   Omni Coliseum, Atlanta, Georgia

December 18, 19   Curtis Hixon Convention Hall, Tampa, Florida

1974

Jerry Garcia begins recording his second solo album, *Compliments of Garcia.*

February 22-24   Winterland, San Francisco, California

March 23   Cow Palace, San Francisco, California

The Dead begin recording *Mars Hotel,* March 25.

May 12   University of Nevada, Reno, Nevada

May 14   Adams Field House, University of Montana, Missoula, Montana

May 17   Pacific National Exhibition Coliseum, Vancouver, Canada

May 19   Memorial Coliseum, Portland, Oregon

May 21   Edmundson Pavilion, University of Washington, Seattle, Washington

May 25   Stadium, University of California, Santa Barbara, California

June 8   Coliseum, Oakland, California

June 16   State Fairgrounds, Des Moines, Iowa

June 18   Freedom Hall, Louisville, Kentucky

June 20   Omni Coliseum, Atlanta, Georgia

Mars Hotel, Compliments of Garcia, and Robert Hunter's *Tales of the Rum Runners* released, June 21.

June 22, 23   Jai-Alai Fronton, Miami, Florida

June 26   Civic Center, Providence, Rhode Island

June 28   Boston Garden, Boston, Massachusetts

June 30   Civic Center, Springfield, Massachusetts

July 19   Selland Arena, Fresno, California

July 21   Hollywood Bowl, Los Angeles, California

July 25   International Amphitheater, Chicago, Illinois

July 27   Civic Center, Roanoke, Virginia

July 29   Capitol Center, Landover, Maryland

July 31   Dillon Stadium, Hartford, Connecticut

August 4, 5   Civic Center, Philadelphia, Pennsylvania

August 6   Roosevelt Stadium, Jersey City, New Jersey

September 9-12   Alexandra Palace, London, England

September 14   Olympia Halle, Munich, West Germany

September 20-22   Palais des Sportes, Paris, France

October 16-20   Winterland, San Francisco, California

1975

The Dead begin recording *Blues for Allah,* January.

Old and In the Way, Keith and Donna, and Robert Hunter's *Tiger Rose* are released, March.

March 23   Kezar Stadium, San Francisco, California—S.N.A.C.K. benefit [as Jerry Garcia and Friends]

June 17   Winterland, San Francisco, California—Bob Fried Memorial Benefit [as Jerry Garcia Band, Kingfish, and Friends]

August 13   Great American Music Hall, San Francisco, California

Blues for Allah is released, September 1.

September 28   Lindley Meadow, Golden Gate Park, San Francisco, California

Phil Lesh and Ned Lagin's *Seastones* is released, October.

1976

Jerry Garcia's *Reflections,* Mickey Hart's *Diga Rhythm Band,* and Bob Weir's *Kingfish* are released, March.

Steal Your Face, a live album from the October 1974 concerts, is released, June.

June 3, 4   Paramount Theater, Portland, Oregon

June 9-12   The Music Hall, Boston, Massachusetts

June 14, 15   Beacon Theater, New York, New York

June 17-19   Capitol Theater, Passaic, New Jersey

June 21-24   Tower Theater, Upper Darby, Pennsylvania

June 26-29   Auditorium Theater, Chicago, Illinois

July 12-14, 16-18   Orpheum Theater, San Francisco, California

August 2   Colt Park, Hartford, Connecticut

August 4   Roosevelt Stadium, Jersey City, New Jersey

September 23   Cameron Indoor Stadium, Duke University, Durham, North Carolina

September 24   William and Mary College, Williamsburg, Virginia

September 25   Capitol Center, Landover, Maryland

September 27   War Memorial Auditorium, Rochester, New York

September 28   Onondaga War Memorial Auditorium, Syracuse, New York

September 30   St. John's Arena, Ohio State University, Columbus, Ohio

October 1   Market Square Arena, Indianapolis, Indiana

October 2   River Front Coliseum, Cincinnati, Ohio

October 3   Cobo Arena, Detroit, Michigan

October 9, 10   Coliseum, Oakland, California

October 14, 15   Shrine Auditorium, Los Angeles, California

December 31   Cow Palace, South San Francisco, California

1977

The Dead begin recording *Terrapin Station,* January/February.

February 26   Swing Auditorium, San Bernardino, California

February 27   Robertson Gym, University of California, Santa Barbara, California

March 18-20   Winterland, San Francisco, California

April 22   The Spectrum, Philadelphia, Pennsylvania

April 23   Civic Center, Springfield, Massachusetts

April 25-27   Capitol Theater, Passaic, New Jersey

April 29, 30   Palladium, New York, New York

May 1, 3-5   Coliseum, New Haven, Connecticut

May 7   Boston Garden, Boston, Massachusetts

May 8   Barton Hall, Cornell University, Ithaca, New York

May 9   Memorial Auditorium, Buffalo, New York

May 11   Civic Center, St. Paul, Minnesota

May 12, 13   Auditorium Theater, Chicago, Illinois

May 15   Arena, St. Louis, Missouri

May 17   Memorial Coliseum, University of Alabama, Tuscaloosa, Alabama

May 18, 19   Fox Theater, Atlanta, Georgia

May 21   Civic Center, Lakeland, Florida

May 22   Sportatorium, Hollywood, Florida

May 25   The Mosque, Richmond, Virginia

May 26   Civic Center, Baltimore, Maryland

May 28   Civic Center, Hartford, Connecticut

June 4   The Forum, Los Angeles, California

June 7-9   Winterland, San Francisco, California

The Grateful Dead movie is released, June.

Terrapin Station is released, July 27.

September 3   Raceway, Englishtown, New Jersey

September 28, 29   Paramount Theater, Seattle, Washington

October 1, 2   Paramount Theater, Portland, Oregon

October 6   University of Arizona, Tempe, Arizona

October 9   McNichols Arena, Denver, Colorado

October 11   Lloyd Noble Center, University of Oklahoma, Norman, Oklahoma

October 12   Armadillo World Headquarters, Austin, Texas

October 14   Hofheinz Pavilion, Houston, Texas

October 15   Moody Auditorium, Southern Methodist University, Dallas, Texas

October 16   Assembly Center, Louisiana State University, Baton Rouge, Louisiana

October 28   Soldiers and Sailors Memorial Hall, Kansas City, Missouri

October 29   Field House, Northern Illinois University, Dekalb, Illinois

October 30   Assembly Hall, Indiana University, Bloomington, Indiana

November 1   Cobo Arena, Detroit, Michigan

November 2   Field House, Seneca College, Toronto, Canada

November 4   Cotterell Gym, Colgate University, Hamilton, New York

November 5   War Memorial Auditorium, Rochester, New York

November 6   Broome County Arena, Binghamton, New York

December 27, 29-31   Winterland, San Francisco, California

1978

Bob Weir's second solo album, *Heaven Help the Fool,* is released, January.

January 6   Swing Auditorium, San Bernardino, California

January 7, 8   Golden Hall, San Diego, California

January 10, 11   Shrine Auditorium, Los Angeles, California

January 13   Arlington Theater, Santa Barbara, California—Stop Nuclear Power benefit

January 14   Civic Auditorium, Bakersfield, California

January 15   Selland Arena, Fresno, California

January 17   Memorial Auditorium, Sacramento, California

January 18   Civic Auditorium, Stockton, California

January 22   McArthur Court, University of Oregon, Eugene, Oregon

January 30-February 1   Uptown Theater, Chicago, Illinois

February 3   Dane County Coliseum, Madison, Wisconsin

February 4   Auditorium, Milwaukee, Wisconsin

February 5   Uni-Dome, University of Northern Iowa, Cedar Falls, Iowa

Jerry Garcia's *Cats Down Under the Stars* is released and the Dead begin recording *Shakedown Street.*

April 6   Curtis Hixon Convention Hall, Tampa, Florida

April 7   Sportatorium, Hollywood, Florida

April 8   Auditorium Coliseum, Jacksonville, Florida

April 10, 11   Fox Theater, Atlanta, Georgia

April 12   Cameron Indoor Stadium, Duke University, Durham, North Carolina

April 14   Coliseum, Virginia Polytechnic Institute, Blacksburg, Virginia

April 15   William and Mary College, Williamsburg, Virginia

April 16   Civic Center, Huntington, West Virginia

April 18   Civic Arena, Pittsburgh, Pennsylvania

April 19   Columbus, Ohio

April 21 Veterans Memorial Hall, Lexington, Kentucky

April 22 Municipal Auditorium, Nashville, Tennessee

April 24 Horton Fieldhouse, Illinois State University, Normal, Illinois

May 5 Thompson Arena, Dartmouth College, Hanover, New Hampshire

May 6 Patrick Field House, University of Vermont, Burlington, Vermont

May 7 Field House, Rensselaer Polytechnic Institute, Troy, New York

May 9 Onondaga War Memorial Auditorium, Syracuse, New York

May 10 Coliseum, New Haven, Connecticut

May 11 Civic Center, Springfield, Massachusetts

May 13 The Spectrum, Philadelphia, Pennsylvania

May 14 Civic Center, Providence, Rhode Island

May 16, 17 Uptown Theater, Chicago, Illinois

June 4 Stadium, University of California, Santa Barbara, California

June 25 Autzen Stadium, University of Oregon, Eugene, Oregon

July 1 Arrowhead Stadium, Kansas City, Missouri

July 3 Civic Center, St. Paul, Minnesota

July 5 Auditorium, Omaha, Nebraska

July 7, 8, August 30, 31 Red Rocks Amphitheater, Morrison, Colorado

September 2 Meadowlands Sports Complex, East Rutherford, New Jersey

September 14-16 Gizeh Sound and Light Theater, Cairo, Egypt—National Antiquities Museum benefit

October 17, 18, 20-22 Winterland, San Francisco, California

November 11 NBC studios, New York, New York—*Saturday Night Live*

November 13, 14 The Music Hall, Boston, Massachusetts
Shakedown Street is released.

November 16-18 Uptown Theater, Chicago, Illinois

November 17 Rambler Room, Loyola University, Chicago, Illinois

November 20 Music Hall, Cleveland, Ohio

November 21 War Memorial Auditorium, Rochester, New York

November 23 Capitol Center, Landover, Maryland

November 24 Capitol Theater, Passaic, New Jersey

December 12 Jai-Alai Fronton, Miami, Florida

December 13 Curtis Hixon Convention Hall, Tampa, Florida

December 15 Boutwell Auditorium, Birmingham, Alabama

December 16 Municipal Auditorium, Nashville, Tennessee

December 17 Fox Theater, Atlanta, Georgia

December 19 Memorial Coliseum, State Fairgrounds, Jackson, Mississippi

December 21 The Summit, Houston, Texas

December 22 Convention Center, Dallas, Texas

December 27, 28 Golden Hall, San Diego, California

December 30 Pauley Pavilion, University of California, Los Angeles, California

December 31 Winterland, San Francisco, California—closing of Winterland

1979

January 5 The Spectrum, Philadelphia, Pennsylvania

January 7, 8 Madison Square Garden, New York, New York

January 10, 11 Nassau Coliseum, Uniondale, New York

January 12 The Spectrum, Philadelphia, Pennsylvania

January 14 Memorial Coliseum, Utica, New York

January 15 Civic Center, Springfield, Massachusetts

January 17 The Coliseum, New Haven, Connecticut

January 18 Civic Center, Providence, Rhode Island

January 20 Shea's Buffalo Theater, Buffalo, New York

February 3 Market Square Arena, Indianapolis, Indiana

February 4 Dane County Coliseum, Madison, Wisconsin

February 6 Fairgrounds Pavilion, Tulsa, Oklahoma

February 7 Arena, University of Southern Illinois, Carbondale, Illinois

February 9, 10 Soldiers and Sailors Memorial Auditorium, Kansas City, Missouri

February 11 Kiel Auditorium, St. Louis, Missouri

February 17 Coliseum, Oakland, California—environmental cancer benefit

Brent Mydland plays in concert with the Dead for the first time, April 22.

April 22 Spartan Stadium, San Jose, California

May 3 Coliseum, Charlotte, North Carolina

May 4 Coliseum, Hampton, Virginia

May 5 Civic Center, Baltimore, Maryland

May 7 Kirby Fieldhouse, Lafayette College, Easton, Pennsylvania

May 8 Recreation Hall, Pennsylvania State University, State College, Pennsylvania

May 9 Broome County Arena, Binghamton, New York

May 11 Forum, Billerica, Massachusetts

May 12 Alumni Stadium, University of Massachusetts, Amherst, Massachusetts

May 13 Cumberland County Civic Center, Portland, Maine

June 28 Memorial Auditorium, Sacramento, California

June 30   International Raceway, Portland, Oregon

July 1   Coliseum, Seattle, Washington

August 4, 5   Auditorium, Oakland, California

August 12   Red Rocks Amphitheater, Morrison, Colorado

August 13, 14   McNichols Arena, Denver, Colorado

August 31   Civic Center, Glens Falls, New York

September 1   Holleder Memorial Stadium, Rochester, New York

September 2   Civic Center, Augusta, Maine

September 4-6   Madison Square Garden, New York, New York

October 24   Civic Center, Springfield, Massachusetts

October 25   The Coliseum, New Haven, Connecticut

October 27, 28   Cape Cod Coliseum, South Yarmouth, Massachusetts

October 29   Capitol Theater, Passaic, New Jersey

October 31-November 2   Nassau Coliseum, Uniondale, New York

November 4   Civic Center, Providence, Rhode Island

November 5, 6   The Spectrum, Philadelphia, Pennsylvania

November 8   Capitol Center, Landover, Maryland

November 9   Memorial Auditorium, Buffalo, New York

November 10   Chrysler Arena, University of Michigan, Ann Arbor, Michigan

November 23, 24   Golden Hall, San Diego, California

November 25   Pauley Pavilion, University of California, Los Angeles, California

November 29   Public Hall, Cleveland, Ohio

November 30, December 1   Stanley Theater, Pittsburgh, Pennsylvania

December 3-5   Uptown Theater, Chicago, Illinois

December 7   Convention Center, Indianapolis, Indiana

December 9   Kiel Auditorium, St. Louis, Missouri

December 10, 11   Soldiers and Sailors Memorial Auditorium, Kansas City, Missouri

December 26-28, 30, 31   Auditorium, Oakland, California

1980

January 13   Coliseum, Oakland, California—Cambodian refugee benefit

March 30-April 1   Capitol Theater, Passaic, New Jersey

April 5   NBC studios, New York, New York—*Saturday Night Live*

April 28   Boutwell Auditorium, Birmingham, Alabama

Go to Heaven is released, April 28; *Jack O'Roses,* Robert Hunter's third solo album, is released, April.

April 29   Fox Theater, Atlanta, Georgia

May 1   Coliseum, Greensboro, North Carolina

May 2   Coliseum, Hampton, Virginia

May 4   Civic Center, Baltimore, Maryland

May 6   Recreation Hall, Pennsylvania State University, State College, Pennsylvania

May 7   Barton Hall, Cornell University, Ithaca, New York

May 8   Civic Center, Glens Falls, New York

May 10   Civic Center, Hartford, Connecticut

May 11   Cumberland County Civic Center, Portland, Maine

May 12   Boston Garden, Boston, Massachusetts

May 14-16   Nassau Coliseum, Uniondale, New York

May 29   Civic Center, Des Moines, Iowa

May 30   Auditorium, Milwaukee, Wisconsin

May 31   Metropolitan Center, Minneapolis, Minnesota

June 5   Compton Terrace Amphitheater, Tempe, Arizona

June 7, 8   Folsom Field, University of Colorado, Boulder, Colorado

June 12   Coliseum, Portland, Oregon

June 13   Center Arena, Seattle, Washington

June 14   Coliseum, Spokane, Washington

June 19-21   West High Auditorium, Anchorage, Alaska

June 29   Pauley Pavilion, University of California, Los Angeles, California

July 1   Sports Arena, San Diego, California

August 16   Edwardsville, Illinois—Mississippi River Festival

August 17   Municipal Auditorium, Kansas City, Missouri

August 19-21   Uptown Theater, Chicago, Illinois

August 23   Alpine Valley Music Theater, East Troy, Wisconsin

August 24   Grand Center, Grand Rapids, Michigan

August 26   Public Hall, Cleveland, Ohio

August 27   Pine Knob Music Theater, Clarkston, Michigan

August 29, 30   The Spectrum, Philadelphia, Pennsylvania

August 31   Capitol Center, Landover, Maryland

September 2   War Memorial Auditorium, Rochester, New York

September 3   Civic Center, Springfield, Massachusetts

September 4   Civic Center, Providence, Rhode Island

September 6   State Fairgrounds, Lewiston, Maine

September 25-27, 29, 30, October 2-4, 6, 7, 9-11, 13, 14   Warfield Theater, San Francisco, California

October 18, 19   Saenger Performing Arts Center, New Orleans, Louisiana

October 22, 23, 25-27, 29-31   Radio City Music Hall, New York, New York

November 26   The Sportatorium, Hollywood, Florida

November 28   Civic Center, Lakeland, Florida

November 29   Alligator Alley Gym, University of Florida, Gainesville, Florida

November 30   Fox Theater, Atlanta, Georgia

December 6   Recreation Center, Mill Valley, California

December 12   Swing Auditorium, San Bernardino, California

December 13, 14   Arena, Long Beach, California

December 26-28, 30, 31   Auditorium, Oakland, California—SEVA benefit, 26

1981

February 26-28   Uptown Theater, Chicago, Illinois

March 2, 3   The Music Hall, Cleveland, Ohio

March 5, 6   Stanley Theater, Pittsburgh, Pennsylvania

March 7   Cole Field House, University of Maryland, College Park, Maryland

March 9, 10   Madison Square Garden, New York, New York

March 12   Boston Garden, Boston, Massachusetts

March 13   Memorial Auditorium, Utica, New York

March 14   Civic Center Coliseum, Hartford, Connecticut

March 20, 21, 23, 24   Rainbow Theater, London, England

March 28   Gruga Halle, Essen, West Germany

Reckoning is released, April.

April 30   Coliseum, Greensboro, North Carolina

May 1   Coliseum, Hampton, Virginia

May 2, 4   The Spectrum, Philadelphia, Pennsylvania

May 5   Civic Center, Glens Falls, New York

May 6, 8, 9   Nassau Coliseum, Uniondale, New York

May 7   NBC studios, New York, New York—*Tomorrow Show*

May 11, 12   Coliseum, New Haven, Connecticut

May 13   Civic Center, Providence, Rhode Island

May 15   Gym, Rutgers University, New Brunswick, New Jersey

May 16   Barton Hall, Cornell University, Ithaca, New York

May 17   Syracuse, New York

July 2   The Summit, Houston, Texas

July 4   Manor Downs, Austin, Texas

July 5   Zoo Amphitheater, Oklahoma City, Oklahoma

July 7   Municipal Auditorium, Kansas City, Kansas

July 8   Kiel Auditorium, St. Louis, Missouri

July 10   Arena, St. Paul, Minnesota

July 11   Alpine Valley Music Theater, East Troy, Wisconsin

July 13, 14   McNichols Arena, Denver, Colorado

Dead Set is released, August.

August 12   Salt Palace, Salt Lake City, Utah

August 14   Center Coliseum, Seattle, Washington

August 15   Coliseum, Portland, Oregon

August 16   McArthur Court, University of Oregon, Eugene, Oregon

August 27, 28   Arena, Long Beach, California

August 30   Compton Terrace Amphitheater, Tempe, Arizona

August 31   Aladdin Theater, Las Vegas, Nevada

September 11-13   Greek Theater, University of California, Berkeley, California

September 25   Stabler Auditorium, Lehigh University, Bethlehem, Pennsylvania

September 26   War Memorial Auditorium, Buffalo, New York

September 27   Capitol Center, Landover, Maryland

September 30   The Playhouse, Edinburgh, Scotland

October 2-4, 6   Rainbow Theater, London, England

October 8   The Forum Theater, Copenhagen, Denmark

October 10   Stadthalle, Bremen, West Germany

October 12   Olympiahalle, Munich, West Germany

October 13   Walter Koebel Halle, Russelsheim, West Germany

October 15, 16   Melk Weg Club, Amsterdam, The Netherlands

October 17   Hippodrome, Paris, France

October 19   Sports Palace, Barcelona, Spain

Bobby and The Midnites, Weir's third solo album, is released, November.

November 29   Civic Center, Pittsburgh, Pennsylvania

November 30   Hara Arena, Dayton, Ohio

December 2   Assembly Hall, University of Illinois, Champaign-Urbana, Illinois

December 3   Dane County Coliseum, Madison, Wisconsin

December 5   Market Square Arena, Indianapolis, Indiana

December 6   Rosemont Horizon, Chicago, Illinois

December 7   Civic Center, Des Moines, Iowa

December 9   Events Center, University of Colorado, Boulder, Colorado

December 12   Fiesta Hall, County Fairgrounds, San Mateo, California—Dance for Disarmament benefit

December 26-28, 30, 31   Auditorium, Oakland, California

1982

February 16, 17   Warfield Theater, San Francisco, California—benefits for Bay Area Causes

February 19, 20   Golden Hall, San Diego, California

February 21   Pauley Pavilion, University of California, Los Angeles, California

March 13   Centennial Coliseum, Reno, Nevada

March 14   Recreational Hall, University of California, Davis, California

April 2 Duke University, Durham, North Carolina

April 3 The Scope, Norfolk, Virginia

April 5, 6 The Spectrum, Philadelphia, Pennsylvania

April 8 Onondaga War Memorial Auditorium, Syracuse, New York

April 9 War Memorial Auditorium, Rochester, New York

April 11, 12 Nassau Coliseum, Uniondale, New York

April 14 Civic Center, Glens Falls, New York

April 15 Civic Center, Providence, Rhode Island

April 17, 18 Civic Center, Hartford, Connecticut

April 19 Civic Center, Baltimore, Maryland

May 21-23 Greek Theater, University of California, Berkeley, California

May 28 Moscone Convention Center, San Francisco, California—Vietnam veterans benefit

July 17, 18 County Fairgrounds, Ventura, California

July 25 Compton Terrace Amphitheater, Tempe, Arizona

July 27-29 Red Rocks Amphitheater, Morrison, Colorado

July 31 Manor Downs, Austin, Texas

August 1 Zoo Amphitheater, Oklahoma City, Oklahoma

August 3 Starlight Theater, Kansas City, Kansas

August 4 Kiel Auditorium, St. Louis, Missouri

August 6 Civic Center, St. Paul, Minnesota

August 7, 8 Alpine Valley Music Theater, East Troy, Wisconsin

August 10 University of Iowa, Iowa City, Iowa

August 28 Veneta, Oregon—Oregon Country Fair

August 29 Center Coliseum, Seattle, Washington

September 5 Glen Helen Regional Park, Devore, California—US Festival

September 9 Saenger Performing Arts Center, New Orleans, Louisiana

September 11 Auditorium, West Palm Beach, Florida

September 12 Civic Center, Lakeland, Florida

September 14 University of Virginia, Charlottesville, Virginia

September 15 Capitol Center, Landover, Maryland

September 17 Cumberland County Civic, Portland, Maine

September 18 Boston Garden, Boston, Massachusetts

September 20, 21 Madison Square Garden, New York, New York

September 23 Coliseum, New Haven, Connecticut

September 24 Carrier Dome, Syracuse University, Syracuse, New York

October 9, 10 Frost Amphitheater, Stanford University, Palo Alto, California

October 17 Downs of Santa Fe, Santa Fe, New Mexico

November 25 Montego Bay, Freeport Zone, Jamaica, West Indies—Jamaica World Music Festival

December 26-28, 30, 31 Auditorium, Oakland, California

The Grateful Dead tour list was first assembled from post-1970 concert contracts by Janet Soto, a member of the band's office staff. It was then refined and considerably expanded by Dennis McNally, a Bay Area-based historian who is working on the band's in-depth biography.

The dates come from many sources—the Grateful Dead news clip collection maintained by Eileen Law at the Dead's office with help from Paul Grushkin, Bill Graham's personal scrapbooks, posters from the collections of Ben Friedman, Tim Patterson, and others, and unpublished interviews with more than a hundred key people. Lou Tambakos, Bob Menke, Dick Latvala, Bob Matthews, Alan Trist, and the members of the Grateful Dead also assisted in the research.

This list is as accurate as serious attention can make it, although we are sure that at least 100 to 200 shows can be added during the years 1966 to 1969. Any corrections, additions, refinements or suggestions should be sent to the authors' attention at the Dead Heads mailing address in San Rafael, California.

Readers of *The Book of the Dead Heads* are heartily encouraged to send their reactions, observations, and additional contributions (stories, photos, artwork) to the Grateful Dead's official Dead Heads mailing address:

Dead Heads
P.O. Box 1065
San Rafael, California 94915

For up-to-date concert information, please use either of the official hotline phone numbers:

West Coast:
(415) 457-6388
East Coast:
(201) 777-8653